D0045288

!

WARNING:

This is a S-L-O-W book. Do not read it while surfing, water-skiing, or running to escape giant weasels. Avoid skimming it while swimming backstroke or speed skating. Please consult a qualified librarian before reading your next book; after this, a fast-paced book might discombobulate your brain.

The SLOW Book

April Pulley Sayre

EST
EVER

WITHDRAWN

Illustrated by **Kelly Murphy**

BOYDS MILLS PRESS
AN IMPRINT OF HIGHLIGHTS
Honesdale, Pennsylvania

Text copyright © 2016 by April Pulley Sayre
Illustrations copyright © 2016 by Kelly Murphy
All rights reserved.
For information about permission to reproduce
selections from this book, contact permissions@highlights.com.

iStock credits: Pages 5 and 60 (dandelion) © rolandtopor;
page 106 (dripping paint) © deystudio;
page 134 (chalkboard) © mysondanube

Boyds Mills Press
An Imprint of Highlights
815 Church Street
Honesdale, Pennsylvania 18431

Printed in China
ISBN: 978-1-62091-783-1
Library of Congress Control Number: 2015953495

First edition
Design by Barbara Grzeslo
Producion by Sue Cole
The text of this book is set in Neutraface Book.
The illustrations are done in pen and ink with digital help.
10 9 8 7 6 5 4 3 2 1

For Rebecca
—APS

To Matryoshka and Émile
—KM

CONTENTS

If you think a table of contents will tell you what is inside so that you can put down the book and not turn a page, you're wrong. This is a slow book, written with snails and sloths in mind.

It may take gumption for you to read it all the way through. But don't worry; this book was manufactured for sampling. Page flipping and rereading are enabled, even encouraged on this device. Read it slowly and you will age.

Here is what you'll find inside in case you're so speedy you cannot wait to discover this book's buried thought potatoes:

- Slow **nature** thoughts—big, chewy thoughts for your brain 8

- Slow **animal** thoughts—creature information sure to slow you to a crawl 24

- Slow **plant** facts—green ponderings to deeply root you 60

- Slow **body** stuff—brain-bouncing bits about your innards 70

- Slow **geology** facts—knowledge to help your forehead fossilize 84

- Slow **stuff**—a rest stop to digest slow food and slow motion 96

- Slow **arts**—the slowest concert in history and tips for watching paint dry 106

- Slow **activities** to try—if you are bold and daring 124

- **Outer space** science—to promote stellar thinking 130

- Two **pages** on which to rest your face as you ponder the slowness of the universe.* 148

- **Chewy words**—a.k.a. the glossary 150

- Excruciatingly slow **acknowledgments** 154

- **Not-exactly-the-end-notes**—extra nourishment for sticky thinkers and snailish sorts 156

- Index 169

---

* These pages are also very good for supporting your head as you watch slugs going about their daily lives.

CHEWY
THO

READ THEM. THINK

SLO

Slow thoughts are often big thoughts

So don't fret if it takes

Don't worry if you need to re

NATURE

UGHTS

ABOUT THEM.

W L Y -

hile to understand them.

em twice.

Traveling in a circle is,
after all,
still traveling.

A GIANT SEQUOIA CAN WEIGH A

BIG TREE

574 BCE Tree began growing

508 BCE Democracy adopted in Athens

44 BCE Founding of the Roman Empire

868 Oldest surviving book was printed, using woodblocks, in China

1088 The first university, the University of Bologna, established

1512 Copernicus claims the sun is the center of our solar system

1663 Cells discovered by Robert Hooke with a microscope

1783 First hot air balloon flight

1824 First dinosaur fossils—for megalosaurus—identified by William Buckland in England

1869 Periodic Table of Elements created by Dimitri Mendeleev

1977 Voyager 1 and Voyager 2 launched to explore Jupiter and Saturn

UCH AS ELEVEN BLUE WHALES.

THOUGHTS

In the Sierra Nevada mountains of California grow giant sequoia trees, *Sequoiadendron giganteum*. These trees can weigh 2.7 million pounds (1.2 million kilograms)—as much as eleven full-grown blue whales. It takes twenty adult humans, holding hands, to reach around a giant sequoia's trunk.

What's even more difficult to wrap one's mind around is the age of these trees. A sequoia can live to be 3,200 years old. Many trees growing in Sequoia and Kings Canyon National Parks have been growing since before the United States became a country. Some have been growing since before the births of the prophet Muhammed, Christ, and even Buddha. Imagine the changes on Earth that have occurred during the lives of these ancient trees. Let those thoughts unfurl, leaf by leaf.

Trees aren't the only long-lived, slow-growing organisms. Deep water black coral (*Leiopathes glaberrima*) can live to be 4,000 years old. Some black corals, alive today, started growing hundreds of years before ancient Egypt's King Tut was born.

Black corals are colonial animals. They are made of hundreds or even thousands of genetically identical, tube-shaped polyps. Polyps are not considered individual animals. So, even if some die, as long as others continue, the overall organism, the colony, survives.

In shallow waters grow coral reefs. A coral reef is made up of many species of coral. As reef-building corals grow, they deposit limestone below them, creating the skeleton of the coral, and, eventually, a reef. Large reef-building corals grow slowly, most adding only a fraction of an inch (a few millimeters) per year, so if you see a large one, it's old.

Reef-building corals also grow in many shapes. Elkhorn coral and staghorn coral form branches shaped like antlers. Brain corals form a dome with a surface pattern that resembles a human brain. (There are many species of brain coral.) The Island of Tobago in the Caribbean has a brain coral that is 16 feet (4.9 meters) in diameter. Depending on its growth rate, it could be anywhere from roughly two hundred to almost a thousand years old. Count to two hundred. Better yet, count to one thousand and let your brain ponder a brain coral lifetime.

SAME GENES BUT NOT THE SAME

A coral colony begins when one polyp attaches to a rock, a sunken ship, or the sea floor. That polyp makes a copy of itself. The new polyp also makes copies of itself—and so on and so on—until there are many, often thousands, of polyps.

Like human identical twins, the polyps all have the same genes. (Genes are the chemical recipes the body uses to grow and repair itself.) Yet some polyps on the same coral can form plate-like structures while others form branch-like shapes. That's because even though they have the same hefty "recipe book" of genes, not all the recipes are followed. Different genes, which determine the polyps' shape, color, and behavior, may be turned on and off during their lives. The local environmental conditions also have a lot to do with the shape of the coral. The same is true of human identical twins. Even though they begin with identical genetic instructions, over time they may become different in height and other features because different genes are activated or inactivated, or each twin's environment is different.

Human twins are individuals. They can live and function separately. Coral polyps grow together and take on different roles so the entire group of thousands acts as one organism.

THE MEMORI

While you're thinking slowly, imagine transforming from a caterpillar into an adult, winged moth. To transform, the caterpillar forms a hardened outer case. This is the pupa stage. (Most, but not all, moths cover this casing with a silk wrapping. The case and silk wrapping are called a cocoon.) Inside this hardened case, the caterpillar's body dissolves to become a soupy liquid. Fortunately, the moth has tiny structures called imaginal discs, which help the soup assemble to form a moth. After the moth's adult body forms, it breaks free of its shell, dries its wings, and flies.

This transformation is so radical, can an adult moth remember anything from its caterpillar days? Biologist Dr. Martha Weiss of Georgetown University wondered about that so she taught tobacco hornworm caterpillars to avoid a stinky gas called ethyl acetate. Then the caterpillars entered their pupa stage. (Tobacco hornworms dig down into soil to pupate. They do not form cocoons.) Finally, the hornworms emerged in their adult, winged form. The moths that had received training avoided the stinky gas. Moths that had not received training did not avoid it. So moths carry some learning from their caterpillar days into their adult, flying form. What else do moths remember about being caterpillars? Chew on that thought until your mind simmers into soup.

S OF A MOTH

A CATERPILLAR ENTERS THE PUPA BOOTH...
...BUT A **MOTH** COMES OUT!

IT'S ABO

Does time fly for a fly? Biologists wonder about this. So you can, too! How long does a minute feel to a mayfly, which may live only one day? How long does a minute feel to a 70-year-old Galápagos tortoise?

Time perception likely depends partly on an animal species' body size. Recent scientific studies hint that smaller animals such as flies experience time in slow motion, compared to the way bigger animals such as humans experience time. (No wonder flies often evade fly swatters. Like fictional superheroes, the flies have seemingly more time to calculate their countermoves and escape.) More study is needed to confirm these differences in time perception across species. Feel free to devote your time to studying this.

HURRY UP! THIS LINE IS LONGER THAN MY LIFE-SPAN!

WAIT A MINUTE

If you are short on houseflies to study, go ahead and examine your own time perception. See how long it takes water to boil. Notice how long an hour lasts when you're having fun or when you're doing something you don't enjoy. Why does time seem to pass so slowly when you're waiting?

Next, ask someone older how time feels to them. (But don't call them old, or ask them what it was like to play with triceratops when they were a kid.) Apparently, the sense of time passing changes as people age.

Find a stopwatch or other timer. Set it for a minute. Ask an

ARE WE THERE YET?

—OR NOT!

older person to tell you, without looking at a clock, when a minute has passed. Ask the same question of a younger person. Scientists actually did this. They found that older people waited more seconds before they said, "A minute has passed!" As humans age, their sense of time passing slows down.

Ironically, this makes older people feel as if time is passing quickly, because a minute elapses long before they realize it has. It makes younger people feel as if time is passing slowly. Now, think about time. Think about it for a long time. That's slow thinking at its finest.

ANOTHER SLOW TH

Decay. Stand and watch an apple turn brown, dry out, shrink, and eventually rot. That should take a few weeks or so.

1700 YEARS AND COUNTING!

IG TO THINK ABOUT:

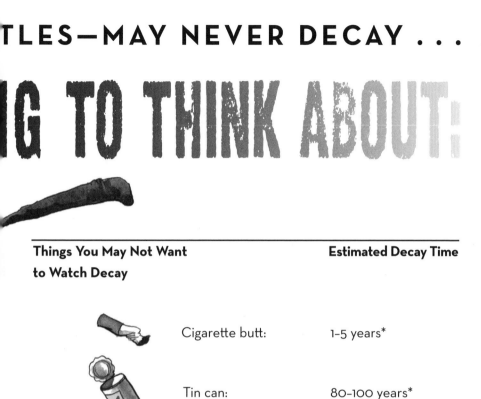

Things You May Not Want to Watch Decay	Estimated Decay Time
Cigarette butt:	1–5 years*
Tin can:	80–100 years*
Aluminum can:	200–500 years*
Glass bottle:	unknown if it ever decays*

*Notice that this list is labeled "Estimated." According to decay expert Darby Hoover, Senior Resource Specialist at the Natural Resources Defense Council, much of this has not been well studied. The problem is that time of decomposition varies according to factors such as moisture, temperature, and exposure to air. So it matters whether the decaying object is in a landfill, a desert, a mucky bog, or the ocean.

Also, it turns out, modern landfills aren't very good spots for decomposition. Most bury and seal off garbage with concrete or compacted dirt. The landfill is essentially a dry tomb, so little decay occurs. (Exposure to rain and air helps things decay.) Garbologists (garbage archaeologists; yes they exist) have discovered 50-year-old intact banana peels in landfills, for example. They can determine age through nearby dated materials like newspapers that also haven't decomposed.

What makes plastic trash problematic is that most plastics humans use were only invented in the last hundred years. No one has ever seen them fully biodegrade—break down into materials normally found in nature. Instead, many plastics break down into smaller plastic pieces, but never stop being plastic. Unfortunately, it's easy for animals to accidentally eat or drink these little pieces, and it's hard to clean them out of streams, lakes, and the ocean.

See where a little scientific list can lead you if you look at it more closely? What if everyone took their science-project time and studied a question related to garbage so we could learn how to dispose of trash in a more environmentally friendly way? Just don't tell your teacher your project is overdue because you are waiting for plastic to biodegrade!

NIMALS

GARDEN SNAIL SPEED:

0.1 inches (2.5 millimeters) per second

Time to cross an 8.5-inch x 11-inch (22 centimeter x 28 centimeter) notebook page: 1 minute, 26 seconds

REAL SNAILS A

Who cares about snails and how they move? Engineer Dr. Anette Hosoi and her colleagues at MIT. Dr. Hosoi and her team found that snails have three kinds of movement. Two kinds involve the snail undulating the underside of its foot. The third type of movement involves the snail picking up the front of its foot and putting it down. In the snail universe, this is basically a gallop. At every speed, the snail squeezes mucus from a gland on its foot. This creates the slippery surface it moves across.

These engineers are studying snails so they can imitate them. (No—Hosoi and her graduate students do not perform the "dance of the snail.") They are working to create Robosnails— robots that move on slime they lay down. Without exposed wheels or legs, Robosnails might be able to travel over rough or hazardous terrain where other robots cannot travel.

ROBOSNAILS

TAKE ME TO YOUR RULER.

TRY A SNAIL'S PACE

Find out what walking at a "snail's pace" means for your local snails. (The speed mentioned earlier was based on a single snail I timed on a warm summer afternoon in Indiana.) Put a snail on a ruler and time how long it takes to cross it. Be sure to clean off the ruler after the experiment. Please also return the snail to wherever you found it. Crawling back home could be a long, slow project for a snail.

IF YOU T

SLOWLY

THE ENT

WORLD C

AMAZING

HINK

ENOUGH,

RE

AN BE

SNAIL THOUGHT:

INCLIN

Snails and slugs are gastropods, which in Latin means "stomach-foot." Ruminate on that name. What would it be like to have a stomach in your foot? Alas, snails do not know the answer, either. Even though the mucus that a snail moves on looks like it could be digestive juice, its stomach is not located there. In a garden snail, the stomach is tucked inside the shell.

They may not have a stomach in that foot, but snails do have an awesome, tongue-like structure called the "radula" at the bottom of it. It is raspy, toothed, scrapes up food, and transports the food in a conveyor-belt-like motion back toward the stomach.

See? People who skim past slow things such as snails miss these intriguing facts. If you think slowly enough, the entire world can be amazing. You can appreciate a thing like mucus. Or leaf stems. Or spittlebugs.

SNAIL-TOOTH STRONG

Scientist Asa Barber, a mechanical engineer, recently tested the strength of those little teeth on a sea snail's radula. (Doesn't everyone wake up with an idea to test sea snail teeth?) Turns out, those teeth are made of the strongest material on Earth. (They beat out spider silk, the previous winner.) They are stronger than a bicycle frame or a bulletproof vest. He hopes to find ways to manufacture this material in order to make stronger, safer products for humans. Again, do not underestimate the snail!

ONE MORE

DO SNAILS MIGRATE? IF THEY DI

HOUSE 4
RENT

A MORE RESEA

Just when you think you're being funny, you discover that someone else takes the whole thing seriously. Right after I had the thought on the previous page, I entered "snail" and "migration" into an Internet search engine. Sure enough, I found articles. Apparently, scientists are trying to find out how snails migrated to mainland Britain ten thousand years ago. By migrate, though, they don't mean that the snails slid all that way. People brought them on purpose, or by accident—inside food, belongings, boats, and so on. Or perhaps snails traveled on logs and other floating debris.

HED THOUGHT

Truth is, land snails are sort of homebodies. On their own power, they do not move very far. Land snail expert Marla Coppolino says "Land snails follow their own slime trails and those of their fellow species in order to not become lost." Coppolino knows her snails; she studies museum snail shells, draws snails for scientific texts, follows snails in nature, surveys snails in wild areas, photographs snails for art, and gives talks to kids and adults about the joys and science of snails. She's also a "snail wrangler" who manages snails on sets for film producers. She is a true celebrant of the slow.

35

THE SLOWEST E-MA

People jokingly call regular mail "snail mail" because it is so much slower than e-mail (electronic mail). Well, I received a real snail mail, carried by a real snail, on November 19, 2009. Alas, it wasn't an envelope on a snail's back. But my husband, Jeff, sent me an e-mail on June 17, 2008, via a service called www.realsnailmail.net. This service is dedicated to slowness. The message took seventeen months and two days and was carried by agent #6, a snail named "Agatha." How did it work? After Jeff sent them an e-mail, a real snail, with transmitters on its back, slowly slimed its way around its cage until it was close enough to transmit its e-mail message to another e-mail service. Then, I received the e-mail. So it was both e-mail and snail mail at the same time.

AMED "AGATHA" . . .

I HAVE RECEIVED

TURTLE: SLOW BUT STEADY WINS THE RACE

In Aesop's fable about the race between the tortoise and the hare, it's clear why the hare should have won.

Hares can reach speeds of 30 miles per hour.

Tortoises move at 0.013 to 0.029 miles per hour. So it takes them more than a day to walk a single mile.

But speed, of course, isn't everything, as the fable demonstrates.

006

THE TAIL WIGGLES EVEN AFTE

SLOW

The slowworm lives in Europe and Asia. It is unclear who gave it this rather unfair name and why. First, it's not a worm. It's a legless lizard. It's not even as slow as a worm. It eats earthworms and slugs. So it must be a little bit faster than them at some point in order to catch them. Or does it just stay still and wait?

So what if slowworms (*Anguis fragilis*) aren't that slow? Let's not hastily dismiss them because this might be the best publicity these pencil-sized beauties ever receive. If you live where they live, kneel down and notice. Check a compost pile or garden for one. Just don't alarm them, or imitate a bird trying to eat them, because the slowworm may then lose its tail. The tail wiggles even after it's detached from the body. This motion likely distracts the predator so the main part of the lizard can escape. But tail loss really is a loss. It takes a lot of energy to regrow a tail, and the lizard doesn't have a good defense until it has grown a new one.

If you're really lucky, you may see a slowworm giving birth. Unlike most lizards, slowworms are ovoviviparous. *OH-voh-vi-VIP-uh-RUS. Ovoviviparous.* Just saying that word forced me to slow down. Ovoviviparous means that instead of laying eggs, eggs hatch inside a slowworm's body; that's why it gives birth to live young.

WOODCOCK

Sure, a peregrine falcon can fly 28 to 60 miles per hour (13 to 27 meters per second), and more than 200 miles per hour (89 meters per second) when it is diving for prey. But who needs that speed? Not the American woodcock, which is often called one of the world's slowest flying birds. These birds feed mostly on earthworms, so there's no need to outfly those. (They also eat centipedes, snails, grasshoppers, crickets, and other small close-to-the-ground grubs.) Woodcocks can actually fly fairly fast during migration. Their really slow flight, 5 miles (8 kilometers) per hour or less, is part of a courtship display.

Each spring, woodcocks gather on open fields as the sun sets. They spiral upward. As they spiral, their feathers make a twittering noise. Then, the woodcocks fly so slowly, their wings stall. A stall occurs when their forward movement is not enough to prevent downward movement, i.e., falling from the sky. As a result, the woodcocks drop to the ground. (Is a bird "good" at flying slowly if it actually falls?) Apparently, all this fancy flying, complete with stalling, is appealing to female woodcocks. Or at least male woodcocks behave as if that is so.

THAT WOULD BE ZE

A VOTE FOF

HOVERING

If you think about it, another slow flier is the hummingbird. It can hover without going anywhere at all. That would be zero miles per hour. Of course, no one ever puts it on a slow list because its wings are moving incredibly quickly in order to keep it hovering. Also, its movement is not considered forward-moving flight, so its magnificent effort does not count.

SLOW WINGS

Over land, turkey vultures have some of the slowest, least frequent, wing beats of all birds. When they're gliding, turkey vultures may flap only a few times an hour. Their flaps are slow and deep compared to other birds. Just a thought: do turkey vultures need to hurry in order to catch up with a carcass?

Cranes, too, are infrequent flappers. They can soar for hours with just a few flaps. One reason large-winged birds, such as cranes and vultures, can avoid flapping for so long is that they hitch rides on upward-moving air. The birds spiral up thermals: huge pockets of air that warm and rise over sunlit fields, parking lots, and cities. After climbing, the birds soar until they lose altitude and find another area of rising air.

THANK GOODNESS THE WORLD IS FULL OF HOT AIR.

44

TH JUST A FEW FLAPS.

BEAT ACROSS CONTINENTS

THERMAL LIFT

SLO

Albatrosses have the largest wings of any flying bird. Their wingspan can be 11 feet (3.5 meters). That's one and a half times as wide as the arm span (arms wide, fingertip-to-fingertip measurement) of a professional basketball player. With long wings, albatrosses can glide for thousands of miles across the ocean without landing. Like vultures and cranes, they may flap only a few times per hour.

These world-class gliders are seemingly unstoppable, yet one thing drags them down: fishing longlines. In a hurry to catch fish, modern fishing boats set lines that are anywhere from 1 mile

BACK AWAY FROM THE BUOY!

WINGS AT SEA

(1.6 kilometers) to more than 50 miles (80 kilometers) with many baited hooks along their length. Albatrosses dip down to eat the bait, become hooked, then drown. Many solutions to this problem have been proposed: coloring the bait to make it less attractive to birds, flying streamers along the lines to startle birds, and weighting the lines so they would sink deeper, away from birds. Setting these lines at night, instead of day, would be a huge help because albatrosses tend to hunt and feed during the day. Could we just, as a world, slow down and save these extraordinary birds?

ST ANIMAL

Would you like to join the debate about which is the slowest animal? The slowest marine animal, according to many science writers, is the sea horse. It moves at 0.01 miles per hour. So it would take 100 hours to travel a mile. But what about coral? Coral polyps are animals, and they hardly shift position at all. Does staying put count as slow? In a way, reef-building corals do move—upward and outward over the years as they build their coral skeleton below them.

TRAFFIC AHEAD

SPEED LIMIT .01

NEMATO

Scoop a handful of soil; you probably have more than a thousand nematodes, also called roundworms, in there. One bright scientist proposes that nematodes are the slowest animals. Racing nematodes might be intriguing. But which ones should you choose? There are over 20,000 nematode species. Nematodes are the most common animals on Earth.

Nematodes are wild, weird, and diverse. Many nematodes are microscopic. Most are harmless, even helpful to humans. Yet some can cause deadly disease in humans, dogs, cats, and crop plants. Scientists found a whopper of a nematode, 27.6 feet (8.4 meters) long, inside a whale!

Intrigued? Then study nematodes, the world's most important worms. You might help save millions of people's lives and help farmers grow healthier crops. (A few whales might be comfier, too.) We'll wait until you time their speeds before adding them to the slow-creature Olympic podium. In the meantime, enjoy other creatures' slow moves in the chart on the facing page.

MORE SLOW CREATURE STATISTICS

Courtesy of Professor Robert McNeill Alexander, who studies animal locomotion:

Sea anemones:	0.01 to 0.3 millimeters/second
Limpets:	about 1 millimeter/second
Tortoises:	60–130 millimeters/second
Protozoans:*	
Amoebas:	about 0.005 millimeters/second or roughly 20 millimeters/hour
Flagellates:	0.02 to 0.2 millimeters/second
Ciliates:	0.4 to 2 millimeters/second

*Note that protozoans are no longer classified as animals so they cannot compete in the slowest animal race. (Protozoans are now considered "protists," which are neither animals nor plants.)

THE MISLEADING

MICROSCOPE

Look through a microscope and you may see tiny creatures zipping around quickly. That can be misleading. As Professor Alexander explains, "Some of them look quite fast when seen through a microscope. But that is only because the microscope magnifies the distance travelled."

SLOW MO

Slowness isn't just about locomotion. It applies to other animal processes as well. A case in point is a deep-sea octopus that lived off the California coast. Most octopuses do not live very long—perhaps a year or two. So Monterey Bay Aquarium research scientists were certainly surprised when their robotic vehicle videotaped a deep-sea octopus again and again, over the course of 53 months. The octopus was clinging to a rock wall 4,500 feet (1,400 meters) below the ocean's surface. She was sheltering eggs. She took care of those eggs for four and a half years. Finally, the robotic explorer vehicle found

the mother octopus gone and her 150 eggs open, presumably hatched. That deep-sea octopus now holds the record for the longest time brooding—taking care of a batch of eggs—of any animal.

COW DIGESTION

We've already covered the slow outsides of animals. But what about slow innards? For slow digestion, take a look at leaf eaters. Leaves are one of the most difficult foods to totally digest. Plant cell walls are sturdy and hard to break down. So, leaf eaters take their time. Sloths spend a lot of time resting, allowing the leaves to digest. Cows swallow leaves, begin digesting them in the first chamber of their four-chambered stomach. Then the leaf wad, called cud,

comes back up into their mouth. They chew it some more. The leaf wad is swallowed again and moves to the cow's other stomach chambers for further digestion.

When cows graze in pastures or eat baled hay, they sometimes accidentally eat bits of scrap metal such as barbs from barbed wire fences. These pieces of metal can scrape the inside of the cow and cut holes in the cow's stomach, a problem labeled "hardware disease." To prevent this problem,

AND OTHER
LOW STOMACHS

farmers feed cows a special kind of magnet. The magnet stays in the cow's stomach. The metal sticks to the magnet. Clumped together on the magnet, the metal pieces do not travel through the smaller passages in the cow's digestive system, so they are less likely to harm the cow. The magnet remains in the cow for its entire life. This has nothing to do with slowness, but it's the kind of lovely, gross fact you are likely to find upon leisurely examination of the world's creatures.

. . . THEY MAY HELP SC

BACI
THANK A SEA SLU

58

NTISTS CURE DISEASES.

TO GASTROPODS: TODAY

People and giant sea slugs share a lot of the same genes, including many of the genes that are suspected to cause Alzheimer's and Parkinson's diseases. (No, sea slugs did not cause these diseases in humans. They just have some of the same genes—those chemical instructions for how the body grows and works.) Because of this similarity between sea slugs and humans, scientists are studying sea slugs. Sea slugs' neurons—nerve cells—are very large. Those cells are easier to study than human nerve cells, which are not only small, but are also located in and connected to people's brains, where poking around and testing things is not generally appreciated. So thank the sea slugs—someday they may help scientists cure diseases.

PLANTS

Plants just sit there, right? Okay, so they don't sit there. They grow there. Yet plants move more than most people realize. Tree trunks grow upward. Leaves expand. Flower buds open. Seedpods pop, explosively throwing their seeds into the air. Winged seeds glide on

DRILS LIKE LASSOS.

wind. Mangrove plants form curved stems that step-by-step grow outward, anchor underwater, and help create a new shoreline.

Much of this motion, though, takes place at speeds too slow for us to notice minute to minute. Some vines, for example, swing their tendrils like lassos. They grab onto other plants and pull themselves upward. But this is hard to see unless you film the plants and then watch the film at a high speed.

THE CENTU

A radish can sprout from seed, grow stems, leaves, and roots, and form a flower and new seeds in just five weeks. A jack-in-the-pulpit plant may need to grow for seven years before it has the energy, stored in its roots, to send up a flower and make seeds. Even slower to mature is the century plant, as its name hints.

Legend has it that the century plant blooms once a century. But the legend is not true. In botanical gardens and on farms, century plants, also called agave plants, can actually bloom in as little as ten to twenty-five years. That still makes this plant sound like a slow bloomer considering that many plants complete this growth in a single year or less. But, as usual, the story is more layered. When the plant is mature, a thick central

stalk shoots up, and a flower forms. That flower stalk can grow 5 to 6 inches (13 to 15 centimeters) taller in a single day. Does that make it a quick bloomer, after all? The stalk can reach a height of 30 feet (9 meters), almost as high as an Olympic high-dive platform. In May of 2014, University of Michigan's Matthaei Botanical Gardens had to take a glass panel out of their greenhouse ceiling to allow their 80-year-old agave plant to flower. After it flowers, the show is over. These plants only bloom once in their lifetime, then they die.

HOW SLOW CAN

Saguaro cacti start slowly and
grow slowly. It takes about fifteen
years before they grow 1 inch (2.5
centimeters) high. It is forty or fifty
years before they reach 10 feet
(about 3 meters) tall and flower
for the first time. At seventy-five
to one hundred years old, saguaro
cacti grow their distinctive side
arms. These plants can live to be
more than 150 years old.

AND EVERYONE
THINKS I'M THE
SLOW ONE!

1 INCH
15 YEARS

1 FOOT
25 YEARS

3 FEET
35 YEARS

THEY GROW 1 INCH . . .

YOU GROW SAGUARO?

10 FEET
50 YEARS

15 FEET
75 YEARS

30+ FEET
150+ YEARS

THE METHUSELAH TREE IS

SLOW SU

Even older than the sequoias—those giant trees that can live 3,200 years—are the short-in-stature Great Basin bristlecone pines (*Pinus longaeva*). One of these pines, nicknamed the Methuselah tree, is almost 5,000 years old. It, and other ancient trees, live at about 10,000 feet, high in California's White Mountains. Up on these mountains, where it's dry, windy, and often cold, trees grow very slowly. The soil is mostly limestone, with very few of the nutrients found in better soils. A tree only a few feet high may be several hundred years old. You can visit the grove of ancient trees, but there is no label on the Methuselah tree. The United States Park Service protects its identity so no one will be tempted to take a piece of bark as a souvenir.

Just imagine how many storm winds have passed through that bristlecone's needles. How many ravens have perched in its branches? How many summer suns and winter moons have helped it cast a shadow on the ground? Do you have to see a thing in person to care that it exists? Or is it enough to know that you share the planet with stately saguaros, century plants, and ancient bristlecone pines?

RVIVORS

IN PURSUIT OF OLD

In her book, *The Oldest Living Things in the World*, Rachel Sussman describes traveling worldwide to see ancient plants. Among the plants she visited were these:

Welwitschia plant, Namib desert, Namibia:	2,000 years old
Moss in Antarctica:	5,500 years old
Mojave yucca in California:	12,000 years old
Rare eucalyptus in Australia:	13,000 years old

I WAS JUST A YOUNG SAPLING WHEN THEY WERE BUILDING THE PYRAMIDS.

69

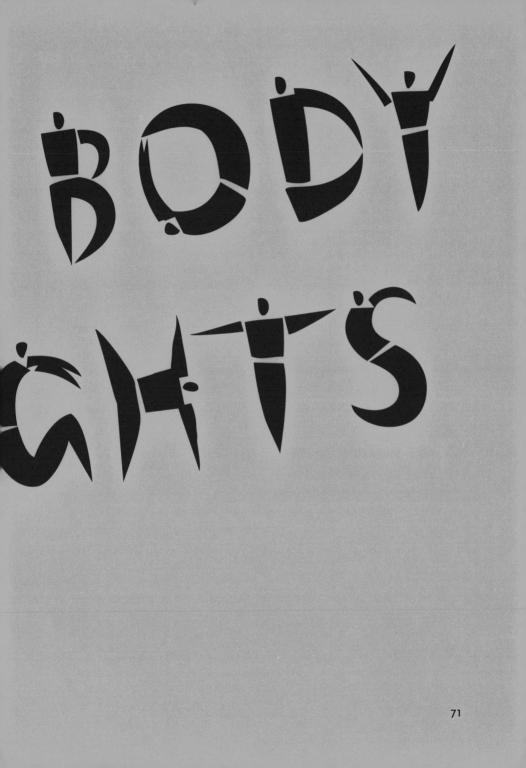

Focusing on yourself isn't always a bad thing. It isn't even rude. You have some awesome machinery in that body of yours. Flex your arm and consider how it works like a lever. Use a magnifying glass or a cell phone camera, zoomed in, to check out those folds on your knuckles. Without their stretch, you couldn't flex your digits. See—saggy, wrinkled skin can be useful. Isn't that "handy"? Take a moment to glance sideways in the mirror and notice how there's plenty of room behind your face. Your head isn't a simple oval as in a flat cartoon. The skull is a brain container, complete with a hard outer shell and fluid to help cushion the brain. (It's too bad that a full helmet is not included for high-impact sports.) Next, try to understand how your brain can think about your brain. Along the way, consider the following slow human body feats.

ME MACHINERY . . .

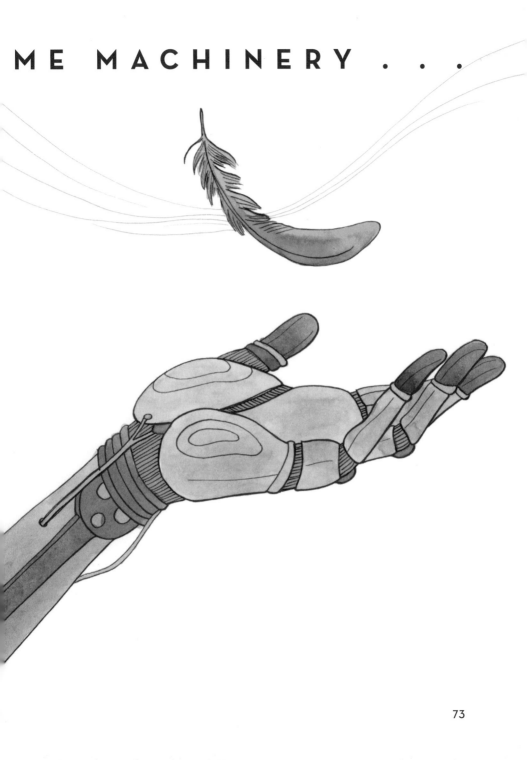

THE OCE

You are mostly water. People are made up of 50 to 70 percent water on average. The amount of water in your body depends on age, exercise, amount of muscle and fat, and whether you are male or female. Muscle tissue contains more water, by weight, than fat tissue. So "leaner" people, such as athletes, tend to have more water per pound or kilogram of body weight.

All the water on Earth has always been here except for water brought by comets. It is constantly recycled. So that water inside your body was once up in a cloud. It may have flowed in the Mississippi River, the Ganges, the Amazon, or the Nile. It probably fell as snow, maybe even in Antarctica. Or it could have been part of an Arctic iceberg, beneath a polar bear.

SNOW

SURFACE RUNOFF

4 THOUGHT

You are a human air conditioner. You change the condition of the air. Scientists estimate that each day you breathe over 23,000 times. Air moves into you. Air moves out of you. You add moisture to the air and exchange oxygen for carbon dioxide.

An adult human moves 300 or so cubic feet (8.5 cubic meters) of air around during all this breathing each day. That's the amount of air inside three midsize automobiles. Whatever your size or age, you move a substantial amount of air, too. Some of the oxygen from air travels in your blood before being pushed back out through your lungs, windpipe, mouth, and nose. You are made partly of air—and air that holds up a kite, that blows in the trees, that ripples a lake, may once have been part of you.

SLOW AND SL

In order to sleep, you have to slow down. You stop moving your arms. You stop moving your legs (unless you're a nighttime kicker). Your breathing slows. Your heart slows. Then you fall asleep. See? Slowing down can be useful.

But does your brain really slow down and rest during sleep? Scientists used to think so. Then they found they were wrong. The brain is quite active during sleep, especially during dreams. It can be as active as it is during the hours you are awake. In a recent study, sleepers were able to correctly push buttons to classify words (read aloud to them) as animal names or object names. Go ahead and wonder what your brain is thinking when you don't know it is thinking because you are asleep.

$$a^2 - b^2 = (a+b)$$

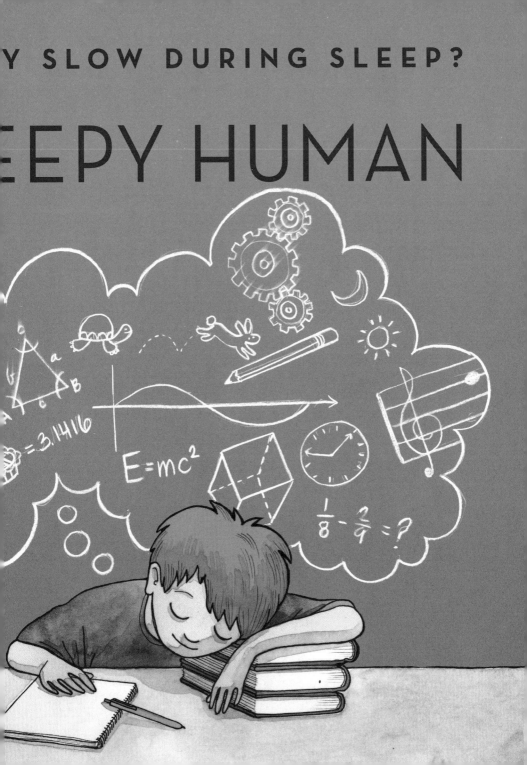

CYCLES OF S

The human body has natural rhythms of activity and rest. Many of these rhythms have a 90-minute cycle. Every 90 minutes or so, a person's need to go to the bathroom may increase. (You don't have to go, but you may feel the urge.) Every 90 minutes or so, your stomach may send messages that you need to eat. Your mouth may also want to chew something, whether that is food, gum, or the end of a pencil. Every 90 minutes, your body also goes through a few minutes when you feel slightly slow and sleepy. If you close your eyes during this time, you're more likely to go to sleep. But if you keep awake during this time, the sleepy feeling will probably pass. Fortunately, all these 90-minute cycles do not coincide; otherwise, you would be sleepy, hungry, and need to go to the bathroom at the same time!

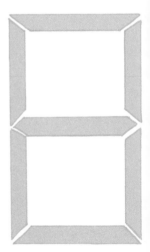

THE SLEEPY

Adults sleep about 8 of every 24 hours. If you live to be 60 years old, you will sleep for about 20 years. You will spend a third of your life asleep. So find a pillow you really like.

LIVES OF
HUMAN BEINGS

SWEAT IT, SLOWLY

Try walking as slowly as you can. (Please do not try this while crossing a street.) You may find slow walking more exhausting than you might imagine. T'ai chi, a kind of martial art, uses slow movements that exercise the body. By working in "slow motion," your muscles have to exert fine control and stabilize your arms and legs. This can be more tiring than walking quickly. Try doing very slow sit-ups. You'll see how hard they are, in comparison to quick sit-ups. T'ai chi and other slow arts such as yoga are great for strengthening your body. Challenge your friends to a slow walk. Moving slowly can, indeed, make you strong!

GEOLOGICAL
THOUGHTS
WORTH
SAVORING

It took six million years for the Colorado River to cut down into rock to form the Grand Canyon. Six million years ... that's 6,000,000 years. That's 60,000 human lifetimes of humans who live to be 100 years old. That's 60,000 box turtle lifetimes. That's a very long time. The Grand Canyon is worthy of a long, slow think.

NOT TOO CLOSE TO THE EDGE, BOB!

SIGNS OF THE

Landmarks seem like they will never change. But the Statue of Liberty, which is covered with copper plates, was originally brown, not green. Over many years, oxygen in the air reacted with the copper statue to form a green patina, a very thin coating that is chemically different from the metal beneath. (How long it took for the Statue of Liberty to form its deep green patina is a matter of debate. Experts suggest about 20 years.)

Early in its history, someone disliked the color change and suggested painting the statue its original color. Fortunately, that idea was discarded because it might damage the statue's patina. This coating helps keep underlying metal from corroding any further. Many people like the look of patina and the protection it offers. So artists often treat the surfaces of metal art with chemicals to immediately create a patina instead of waiting for natural patina to form.

ORIGINALLY BROWN . . .

TIMES: PATINA

MOUNTAIN W

Exposed to very little pollution,
a mountain of hard granite
should erode only about 1 inch
(2.5 centimeters) in 10,000 years.
But no one has watched this entire
process in action. It would be
helpful if someone would study
this, in person. Any volunteers?

GRAVEYA

Most people visit graveyards to celebrate loved ones or study human history. Scientist Tom Meierding goes to study rocks. The great thing about tombstones as rock samples is that tombstones have dates on them. The dates indicate when a person died. But they also indicate when the tombstone was cut and placed. Meierding studies weathering: the long slow process of rocks wearing down and breaking apart over time. The death date on a tombstone indicates roughly when a tombstone's cut rock face was first exposed to air and precipitation and began weathering.

Most new tombstones are even in thickness. Engraved letters are deep. Over time, air pollution such as acid rain dissolves rock, especially marble. The lettering becomes shallower. The more

exposed part of the rock, near the top, thins. The part near or below the dirt, protected from air, remains thick.

Meierding and other scientists measure the thickness of the tombstone from top to bottom and the depth of lettering. Using these measurements, and controlling for a few factors such as the kind of rock, Meierding can find out when and where weathering is rapid. He found heavy rates of weathering in graveyards near industrial areas that burnt a lot of coal, especially in the decades before air pollution laws were enacted. Those gravestones sometimes thinned by more than one-tenth of an inch (3 millimeters) every century. Students as far away as Australia are using his technique to study rock weathering via measuring tombstones.

WATCH THE "ATLAN

Earth's continents and ocean basins ride on tectonic plates—vast pieces of the Earth's crust that move. In the center of the Atlantic Ocean is the Mid-Atlantic Ridge, where the North American plate and the Eurasian plates are pulling apart. Here, molten rock from deep in the earth pushes to the surface. It spills out and hardens, forming new crust. Most of the Mid-Atlantic Ridge is underwater. But at Thingvellir, Iceland, you can actually see the Ridge on dry land. Each year, the Atlantic Ocean widens by about an inch (2.5 centimeters). That is about the speed at which your fingernails grow. This may seem slow. But for a geological process, it's quite rapid.

HELLO, EUROPEANS!

SLOW

Modern life is full of
fast movers: race cars,
jet planes, and bullet trains.
Fast answers, fast food, and

STUFF

WHOA

fast-loading websites are celebrated. But not everyone is on board. Some folks are saying, "Whoa!"

N O   M O R E
S L O W

You've probably heard of fast food: food that's made quickly and handed out from drive-through windows. Fast food can be tasty. It can be quick. But groups of people all over the world have started a revolt against it. They want a return to locally grown varieties of food prepared slowly and enjoyed slowly. No more gulping! No more scarfing it down! These folks created an organization called the Slow Food Foundation for Biodiversity. Their mission is to celebrate the delicious, healthy variety of food grown and eaten by people all over Earth, instead of the always-the-same food of fast-food restaurants.

YOUR RAISINS WILL BE READY IN ABOUT THREE WEEKS, SIR.

G U L P I N G !

F O O D

Time it takes to cook a McDonald's burger: 38 seconds

Average time from order taken to delivery of

     food to customer: 1.5 minutes

Time it took to find this out from a

     local McDonald's: 10 seconds*

*Employees at McDonald's take pride in shaving seconds off the time it takes to process an order. So the person who answered the phone knew right away what average they were running. Your local restaurant may have a slightly different time.

Time it takes to cook Italian spaghetti sauce in

     a 5-quart (4.7 liter) slow cooker: 8 to 9 hours

Time it takes to make a raisin from a grape: 3 weeks*

*The grapes are set out on trays in the sun and left to dry for the entire 3 weeks. Sun-dried raisins are dark in color. It takes 4.5 pounds (2 kilograms) of grapes to make 1 pound (half a kilogram) of raisins.

Time it takes to make sauerkraut by an

     old-fashioned recipe: 3 to 4 weeks*

*Five pounds of cabbage is shredded, soaked in salt and sugar, and left to ferment in a crock or bucket in the ground. Now that's slow food.

SLOW M

Slow motion is a technique used in films and video. It appears to "slow down" an action. Slow motion can reveal details of movement. For instance, a sports trainer might show an athlete a slow-motion film of his or her golf swing, batting style, running style, or diving style. Then athletes can make small adjustments to their movements to improve their success.

Slow motion, ironically, is created by shooting pictures at faster speeds. Normally, film or video is created by taking many still pictures (frames) of whatever is happening. These still pictures are played back rapidly so that our eyes see them as continuous motion. Film is typically shot in 24 frames per second. Video is generally shot in 30 frames per second.

To make slow motion, a camera must shoot more than 24 or 30 frames per second. Then, the multiple frames are played back at regular speed. This stretches out the action so we perceive it as moving more slowly.

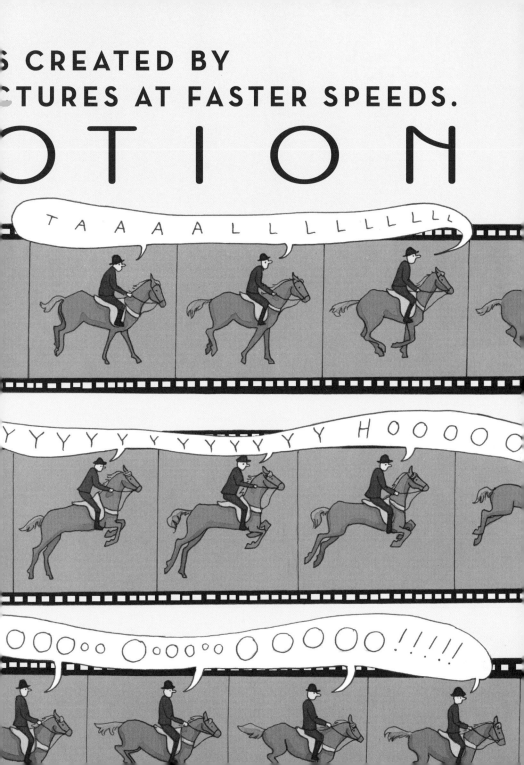

THE MOONWA

Ornithologist (bird scientist) Kim Bostwick uses a high-speed video camera to study birds. Her camera can take 500-1000 frames, or pictures, per second. She took a video of the display of several species of manakins, birds that live in Central and South America. The male manakins hop from branch to branch and make wing sounds to impress females. These sounds include various pops, clicks, snaps, and hums. Most of the action is so fast, it's impossible for humans to see. By videotaping the birds at high speeds, and then slowing

⌐KING BIRDS

down the tape for slow-motion playback, Bostwick discovered that club-winged manakins create sounds by lifting their wings above their heads and smacking and rubbing them together. Her high-speed video played back in slow motion also revealed the extraordinary display of red-capped manakins. These birds perform a courtship ritual with fancy footwork that looks a lot like the "moonwalk" dance move made famous by Michael Jackson.

ARED A SLOW DAY."

HOUGHT

What if, instead of snow days, we had slow days? You wake up one morning and the radio says, "Today has been declared a slow day." Everyone could walk slowly. They might see things they have never seen before. Everyone could eat slowly. People would read and wander. You could take forever to pick up the grimy socks from the floor of your room. You could talk with a slow-motion voice to your parents. What else would happen on a slow day? Slow down and imagine that for a while.

ART

In February, 2003, in Halberstadt, Germany, a concert performance of the slowest piece of music began. The composition, called "As Slow as Possible," is being played on a church organ and will last approximately 639 years. The first year and a half of the piece was silent because the music began with a rest. "As Slow as Possible" was composed by John Cage, who did not live to hear it played.

Cage can't be blamed for the full slowness of the work. He wrote it to be twenty minutes or so long. But some philosophers and musicians decided to make the music match Cage's title exactly, so they are playing it more slowly. There's no need to rush to this particular concert. You can probably wait until you grow up, have a career, and even retire before you fly to Germany to savor it.

Other composers are reportedly working on pieces that will last a thousand years. So, which will be the slowest and longest-lasting concert? It depends on who can gather enough musicians—or computers—to keep on playing, century after century.

. . . SOME FOLKS MIGHT

WATCHING

PAINT DRY

A common expression for something boring is that it is "as exciting as watching paint dry." The assumption is that paint drying is a long, slow process. But is it?

How long paint drying takes depends on the paint. Latex wall paint can dry enough in one to four hours so that you can add another coat of paint. In contrast, oil-based wall paints may need twenty-four hours before it's safe to add a second coat.

It can take several weeks for traditional oil paints, used in fine art paintings on canvas, to "set to touch," so you can touch them with your finger without disturbing the surface paint. Oil paint is basically pigment—the color—suspended in oil. Linseed oil, walnut oil, poppy seed oil, and safflower oil can all be used. How long a painting takes to dry depends on what kind of oil, and how much of it, is used in the paint. Paint drying speed also depends on surrounding air temperature and humidity. Paint typically dries faster in warmer, drier air. Some oil paintings take years to dry. Also, because there is still oil in the paint, some folks might never consider it "dry." Acrylic paint was invented in the 1940s as an alternative to traditional oil paint. Acrylic paint, also used on canvas, can dry in eight to twenty-four hours. (Many artists still choose traditional oil paints, even with the long drying times.)

So, who cares how long it takes paint to dry? Painters, and also paint companies. As a technical manager at a painting company, AquaTec Coatings, Keith Jackson actually had a job watching paint dry. He had to time the drying rates of paints the company sold. (He insisted the job wasn't as boring as it sounded.) He has since retired. Wonder what he does now to relax?

SLOWLY SH

Bonsai are small, potted trees, carefully sculpted for beauty. They are forced to grow slowly. They are usually less than three feet (a meter or so) tall. Bonsai trees are not a special dwarf tree species. They are regular plum, pine, camellia, azalea, and other tree and shrub species that would normally grow ten, twenty, forty, or even a hundred feet tall. The plants are pruned—branches cut to retain the small shape. Their pruning, wiring, watering, fertilizing,

PED: BONSAI

and repotting is done meticulously to maintain the slow, controlled growth of the tree in a relatively small pot. These tiny trees can live for hundreds of years and are treasured within families. They may be passed down from generation to generation. The Bonsai art form originated over a thousand years ago in China and spread to Japan, Korea, and elsewhere.

YOUR GREAT-GRANDFATHER GREW THAT FROM A SEED!

SLOW SC

Usually if you start a project, you should finish it. But sometimes that's not possible in one lifetime. In 1948, Korczak Ziolkowski began carving the Crazy Horse Memorial, a sculpture made of a mountain.

Crazy Horse is a famous Native American warrior. The sculpture depicts both him and his horse. The completed carving will be 641 feet (195 meters) by 563 feet (172 meters) high. It will be taller than a fifty-story building. The original sculptor died in 1982, but his family and others continue his work. When will it be finished? No one knows.

The Crazy Horse sculpture is much taller than the also-famous stone sculptures of Mount Rushmore. Those sculptures, of Presidents George Washington,

Thomas Jefferson, Theodore Roosevelt, and Abraham Lincoln, were carved from 1927 to 1941.

Carving a mountain takes a long time. But what if you make a mistake? That can really slow you down. Thomas Jefferson's head was originally to the left of George Washington's. But after eighteen months of work on the head, the sculptors found that the rock was cracked and unstable. So they blasted his head off the mountain and started his head again, this time in between George Washington and Theodore Roosevelt's faces. Both Mount Rushmore and the Crazy Horse Memorial sculpture are carved into the Black Hills of South Dakota.

JILDING

In the late 1380s, Archbishop Antonio da Saluzzo began building a cathedral in Milan, Italy. He never saw his building finished. But people kept working on it—through the 1400s, 1500s, 1600s, and 1700s. Many architects and powerful people added their own touches to the cathedral, called the Duomo of Milan. In the 1800s, Napoleon Bonaparte put his craftsmen to work on it, too. It wasn't until January 6, 1965, that the last major piece of the Duomo of Milan was completed. Of course, the cathedral is so old, that parts of it are now being renovated. So really, the building and rebuilding never stops.

ANOTHER LON

The Great Wall of China was a long slow build. Work on it began sometime in the third century BCE and lasted about two thousand years. Although it's called "the wall," it's actually a series of overlapping walls and earthen fortifications. Until recently, the wall was estimated to be about 5,000 miles (8,047 kilometers) long. By that measurement, the wall could stretch from South Carolina to California and back. But then the Chinese government spent five years surveying and measuring the wall. In 2012, they announced that the Great Wall is longer than previously thought. According to this new study, its path stretches 13,170.69 miles (21,196.18 kilometers). Less than 10 percent of it remains intact.

G SLOW PROJECT: THE GREAT WALL OF CHINA

IF IT WERE STRAIGHT, THE GREAT WALL WOULD CIRCLE MORE THAN HALF THE EARTH.

SLOW

Television is surely one of the zippiest, quickest forms of media. It has fast cuts between scenes, fast talk, many short segments, and short commercials. Plus you can quickly change channels if a television show lags for a moment.

Yet even in the television business, slow is starting to make a comeback. Norway's public broadcasting station has started to produce "slow TV." In 2009, they showed a seven-hour documentary that chronicled a train trip. Every mile. With cameras mounted on the train. In 2013, they showed eighteen hours of salmon in a stream. On a twelve-hour show called "National Firewood Night," all the techniques and joys of cutting and prepping firewood were described, and the evening featured hours of nothing more

than footage of logs burning. The slow television programs have been quite popular, so the channel has plans to produce more.

SALMON IN A STREAM

124

NGS
TO TRY

TELL A SLOW STORY

1. Decide what your story is about, who your characters are, and what happens in your story.
2. Take forever to tell your listeners any of the things in #1.

SLOW
MOTIONS

Use these words to make your own slow sentences, poems, or stories:

crawl	shuffle
creep	plod
dawdle	drag
dally	lumber
dillydally	linger
trudge	lag
waddle	mosey
saunter	amble
stroll	traipse

IMAGINARY SLOW-MOTION MOVIES

Feel free to make up your own.

When Sloths Attack

When Sloths Attack II: Ten Hours Later

The Slug Who Climbed Mount Kilimanjaro

Moss Growing: A Documentary

Waiting for Ketchup

Weathering: A Rock's Story Three Thousand Years in the Making

How to Count Sheep Effectively

The Return of Molasses: Another Sticky Day

Watching Toenails Grow: The Music Video

Trees: That Oak Was One Little Nut, the Story Ring By Ring

A HODGEPODGE OF

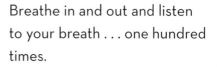

Count the grains of sugar in each of ten teaspoons. See if they all have the same amount.

Catch snowflakes until you find two that are exactly alike.

In autumn, stand by a ginkgo tree and wait until the moment when its leaves fall. (Unlike most trees, ginkgoes tend to lose their leaves almost all at once.)

Count from one to infinity. If you can't finish the job, grow up and have children and ask them to continue the job for you.

Breathe in and out and listen to your breath . . . one hundred times.

Gather pennies until you have one hundred dollars' worth. Then arrange them in rows.

Plant an acorn and keep an eye on it until it becomes a tall tree. If you move to another place, leave a letter for the people who come after you. Tell them when you planted the acorn and ask them to keep measuring the tree.

Devote your life to studying sea sponges, surely some of the slowest and most underappreciated blobs on Earth.

LOW ACTIVITIES

Choose something to study—
perhaps something few other
people have studied.
Begin studying it. Study it
today. Study it a little bit
every day after that. Even if
you grow up to have some
other job, you could still study
your subject a little every
week. You could contribute
to people's knowledge about
your subject. You could expand
other people's thinking. It's a
long, slow process, but very
satisfying.

Make a paper sculpture taller
than a basketball star.

Go out at night and see if you
notice the stars and planets
changing position.

Watch the sunset—every
evening for your entire life.

HTS:
R SPACE

Now that you've had plenty of slow-thinking practice, you should be ready. I've saved some bigger-than-the-galaxy thoughts for last.

WE ARE SEEING LIGHT THAT LEFT
LINGERING OV

ER LIGHT-YEARS

At night, when you look at a star, you're seeing into the past. Those stars are so far away, their light takes a long time to reach Earth and our eyes. When we look at Proxima Centauri, the second closest star, we see light that left it 4.24 years ago. When we view a star such as the North Star, which is 434 light-years away, we are seeing light that left it 434 years ago, light that is just now reaching our eyes. So, when we view Eta Carinae, 7,500 light-years away, we see light that left that star 7,500 years ago. The only star whose light reaches us in under a light-year is the sun, which is our closest star. Its light reaches us in a speedy eight minutes and twenty seconds. (But you shouldn't be staring at it anyway, because that can damage your eyes.)

LIGHT-YEARS BY THE NUMBERS

How far away is a light-year, in miles or kilometers? You can calculate it this way:

Light travels at 186,000 miles (300,000 kilometers) per second.

That speed is multiplied by the number of seconds in a minute (60)

times the number of minutes in an hour (60)

times the number of hours in a day (24)

times the number of days in a year (365).

The total, rounded up, is 6,000,000,000,000 miles. That is 6 trillion miles or about 10 trillion kilometers. Stare at those zeroes for a while and you'll realize why astronomers use light-years to describe vast distances in space. The numbers are so big, in miles or kilometers, that it is difficult for the human mind to grasp their enormity.

6,000,000

186,000

x 60

x 60

x 24

x 365

_____

000,000

DIMMER T

The Hubble Space Telescope can detect much dimmer objects than can be seen with the naked eye. It can detect light produced by deep space objects billions of light-years from us. So it can see into the past, billions of years ago. Why not look upward, even if you're staring at an indoor ceiling? Reach the tendrils of your mind into what happened back then. (You could also stare at the floor. After all, we are riding on a planet. Down below that floor is the Earth, and on the other side of Earth is outer space, too!)

TAKE A REALLY
THE VOY

When Voyager 1 and Voyager 2 were launched in 1977 to explore Jupiter and Saturn, their missions were to last four years, twelve years at the most. But as of March 2015, over 37 years later, these probes were still traveling outward and sending messages back to Earth. They have encountered the outer reaches of the solar system and are exploring interstellar space—more than 12 billion miles from our sun. It takes more than 18 hours for signals from Voyager 1 to reach Earth. (The website www.voyager.jpl.nasa.gov/where/ counts off an updated distance to the probes.) Imagine the things these spacecraft have seen on their voyage. Better yet, study science for the next eighteen years and become an astrophysicist. Because it will take that long, if not longer, to understand all the information Voyager 1 and Voyager 2 have captured.

Our sun and planet Earth are located in a thin disk of stars and planets called a galaxy. Because we are in this galaxy, we cannot see its spiral shape. (You would have to be above or below it to see that shape.) When we look at the sky, we look right through the materials of the disk. That material is the Milky Way.

In 2014, scientists at Cornell University estimated that the conditions needed for complex life to develop exist in at least 100 million places in our own Milky Way Galaxy. By complex life, they mean organisms larger and more intricate than microbes. Consider that the

Milky Way Galaxy is just one of hundreds of billions of galaxies in the Universe. Each of those galaxies has billions of stars. These galaxies have planets, too. At least some of them likely have Earth-like conditions.

OUR SPIRAL

EVELOP EXIST IN 100 MILLION PLACES . . .

GALAXY

What does this have to do with slowness? Well, finding out what, if anything, lives on other planets is a huge project. Part of the problem is that space travel is currently too slow for us to reach places within a single human lifetime. Many brains will need to come together in a long slow think to figure out how to send probes to other planets or how to learn from any signals we receive from outer space. This will be a good job for bold thinkers and mechanical tinkerers, people who will hang on and work even after something fails or after they find their first ideas are wrong. Figuring out what's out there will, without doubt, take a long time and intense study.

The hard part of looking
for life isn't just finding answers.
It's asking the right questions!

WHAT KIND OF **LIFE-FORMS** MIGHT
ARISE ON THESE OTHER PLANETS?

HOW WILL WE **KNOW**
LIFE IS THERE?

WHAT **TESTS** SHOULD
SCIENTISTS RUN?

WHAT COUNTS AS
LIFE?

Draw the life-forms you
imagine on paper or in your mind.
Perhaps sketch out a contraption
to detect them, as well. Better yet,
study to become an astrobiologist,
a scientist whose job is to do this
kind of imagining in a scientific
manner!

If the question of whether there is life on other planets does not slow down your bicycle and your brain, consider this instead: the universe is made of stuff and we don't know what it is. Astrophysicist Dr. James S. Sweitzer puts it this way:

> The type of matter that we are made of (carbon, oxygen, etc.) is a VERY minor constituent of the universe, and only amounts to about 5% of the total . . . Most of the universe is made up of what is called 'dark energy' and 'dark matter.' They are called dark because we can't detect them using light waves and they don't emit light. Yet we have many lines of evidence showing they exist. So, we're at a point in time where well over 95% of the universe is made up of something and we don't know what it is. This is a great mystery.

See why we need you and your brain, at work? Humans have a lot of thinking and studying to do. As a species, we have unanswered questions so big and important that most people cannot manage to keep them in their brains while doing daily tasks such as chopping vegetables, performing dentistry, or flying planes. (Although, I bet it's difficult not to think about universe questions when you are a plane pilot and see the clouds and sky and stars beyond.) For your safety, thinking about outer space life and dark matter while doing these activities really is not recommended. That warning label at the book's beginning was not entirely a joke.

While you're *carefully* thinking big, slow, chewy thoughts, here's one more thing to investigate:

The universe is expanding . . .

-and expanding . . .

Will

your

mind

expand

with

it?

THESE ARE
ON WHICH

This book has breathed all its thoughts out into the galaxy. It is winding down. So let your brain do so, too. Feel free to rest on this book as you look at the sky, or the undersides of chairs.

Mayhap mull over the mysteries of inner ears or dark matter. Ponder periwinkles or moths that live on sloth fur.

PUT YOU

THE PAGES TO REST

Let this book support your chin
as you study butterfly feet
or breathe in sync with a
muddy garden toad.

HEAD HERE

THE END

CHEWY WORDS
(A.K.A. THE GLOSSARY)

Here are words used in the book that were not explained in the text:

acid rain—rain, snow, sleet, fog, or dry particles in the air that have been acidified by pollution. Acid rain can erode sculptures and stone buildings. It endangers the health of trees, fish in lakes, and people's lungs. Most acid rain is caused by pollution from coal-burning power plants and exhaust from cars, trucks, and buses.

Alzheimer's disease—a medical condition that causes memory loss

architect—a person whose job is designing buildings

astrobiologist—a person whose job is studying life in the entire universe, not just on Earth

astrophysicist—a scientist who studies outer space, also known as coolness

biodegrade—a process by which something decays into matter that occurs naturally on Earth

biodiversity—a measure of how many different species inhabit a place

cell—a small unit of life held together by a membrane

ciliate—a complex single-celled organism covered with short hair-like structures called cilia. The cilia beat rapidly. They help the organism move and gather food.

cocoon—a silk-wrapped chamber where moths transform from caterpillars to their adult, winged form

colonial animal—a form of life that contains individuals so interconnected that scientists consider them one organism. Corals, mosses, and Portuguese man-of-wars are all colonial animals.

comet—an outer space object, made of ice and dust, that may form a long tail as it travels

composer—a person who writes music

crust—the outer layer of the Earth. It rides over the Earth's more liquid layer, the mantle. (Note: some people consider the atmosphere, not the crust, the outer layer of Earth. Still other people don't consider anything crust unless it is on an apple pie. Well, like the Earth's crust, an apple pie's crust rides on a hot, semiliquid layer. But one of these two kinds of crust is kinder to your teeth.)

decomposition—the process by which garbage, dead plants, and dead animals break down into smaller parts until they become soil

discombobulate—to baffle or confuse

engineer—a person who uses science and math to study and design systems and structures, from bridges to biological cells

ferment—a process by which yeast or other microorganisms chemically change the natural sugars or starches in food, creating lactic acid, acetic acid, alcohol, or carbon dioxide. This process is used to make pickles, sauerkraut, wine, cheese, and yeasted bread.

flagellate—a microorganism that has a whiplike appendage

garbologist—a scientist who studies trash to learn about the humans who left it and the science of decay

gastropod—a scientific name for a group of mollusks that includes land snails, cowries, whelks, limpets, among others. Most gastropods move on one big muscular foot. Many have spiral shells, but some, such as slugs, do not even have a shell. Gastropods live on both land and in water.

gene—a segment of DNA (deoxyribonucleic acid) or RNA (ribonucleic acid) that provides information to make the building blocks of an organism. In this way, a gene influences the traits of an organism.

geological—having to do with the study of rocks, soil, or landforms

ginkgo—an ancient Chinese tree with fan-shaped leaves which has been widely planted in cities. Like the coelacanth, it is considered a "living fossil" because the species has remained unchanged for millions of years. Modern ones look just like 200 million-year-old fossilized ones.

gland—an organ or group of cells (in the body) that produces and releases helpful liquid, such as saliva or sweat

innards—informal word for inner organs. (By "innards," people almost always mean a slimy pile of intestines, kidneys, and liver, not a tidy blob of heart or lungs.) Innards are also called "viscera." Have you noticed that the expressions "visceral" and "gut feeling" both come from slimy intestine words (viscera and guts)? Yet they both refer to deep inner feelings. Does that mean our deep inner feelings live in our intestines? Hmm—see what fun I had tracing down a word?

interstellar space—the area in between star systems. It is mostly empty space, with an occasional cloud of gas and dust.

kilometer—a unit equaling .62 miles, or about six-tenths of a mile

librarian—the heart of a school or other community, the person whose work energizes circulation, constantly refreshing the flow of knowledge among readers, writers, educators, classrooms, and curious beings, in general. The folks who help human minds cross time and space to learn and cross-pollinate ideas. Also known as: the best chance the human race has of getting smarter over time and not repeating mistakes.

locomotion—self-propelled movement from one location to another

mangroves—any one of four species of shrubs and trees that grow outward along coasts in salty water and help form new land. Mangrove swamps are important nurseries for young coral reef fish, crabs, and wading birds.

matter—a physical substance that takes up space and has mass. Solids, liquids, and gases are all matter, yet energy is not.

mature—fully grown

microscopic—anything difficult to see without a microscope

migrate—to make a yearly, seasonal journey from one place to another and back

moisture—liquid, something wet

mollusk—a member of the phylum Mollusca, a group of animals which have soft bodies and no backbones. Most—but not all—have a fleshy foot and a hard outer shell. Clams, oysters, land snails, octopuses, and squid are all mollusks.

molten rock—rock so hot it has become a liquid

mucus—slippery fluid produced by glands. Snails lay down mucus to help them glide across surfaces. Note that the mucus in human noses does not help people travel across slippery surfaces. But it does protect the lungs. When you inhale, the mucus in your nose catches bacteria, dirt, and other pollutants before they reach the lungs. It even has antibodies to fight disease.

mull—to ponder or think about something for a while. Note that the other meaning is "to mix thoroughly" and this is a good way to think about mulling.

ocean basin—the bottom of the ocean, not including the highest parts (the continental shelves) or the lowest parts (the deepest trenches)

organism—an individual living being

ornithologist—a person who studies birds as a scientific job. Lots of other people study birds just for fun. These are called birdwatchers or birders. Birdwatchers and birders are intriguing people who generally love nature. Some hang out and watch moths, because, if you like birds, hey, why not study moths, or trees, or all the other things that birds need and that need birds?

Parkinson's disease—a nervous system condition that causes muscle weakness

periwinkle—a type of sea snail

polyp—a tiny tube-shaped individual, often part of a coral colony

ponderings—an invented word that is not in the dictionary but that makes this book's author imagine a big messy stack of writing. There is a real word, *ponder*, which means to think about deeply.

protozoan—a tiny, single-celled organism such as an amoeba. Scientists group protozoans, slime molds, and single-celled algae into a group called "protists." The group "protists" is like a scientific junk drawer. Scientists dump puzzling organisms in the "protists" group for now, until they figure out where they should go in classification. Protists aren't animals, plants, or fungi so they don't fit into any of those other handy cabinets/classifications.

reference librarian—see librarian. Then imagine being on call—on the phone and at a desk—for every question on Earth. Also add that you need to have superpower skills to know what resources would help a person find an answer to their question, whether it is about snail teeth, or how to make a soufflé, or where to find a lawyer.

rest (music)—a symbol for a pause during which no notes will be played

snail—one of the world's most fabulous, unheralded creatures, about which entire books should be written daily. Also: a common name for a spiral-shelled mollusk. There are thousands of snail species. They live on land, in rivers, lakes, and the ocean.

solar system—a star and the planets and other objects that orbit around it

species—a kind of animal, plant, or other organism. The human species goes by the scientific name *Homo sapiens*.

t'ai chi—Chinese exercise system that emphasizes slow, controlled movement

tendril—a slender structure a plant stem uses to reach out and attach itself to things

tinkerer—a person who conducts many experiments to adjust or change things while trying to improve something

unfurl—to unroll, usually refers to leaves

EXCRUCIATINGLY SLOW ACKNOWLEDGMENTS

I would like to thank a true teacher, my father, David Pulley. I would like to thank every other teacher I've had, especially Mary Lasher, Barbara Ottewell, Mrs. Joye, Steve Wainwright, Patricia Wright, and Mrs. Paouris.

I would like to thank my editor, Rebecca Davis, who loved, shaped, and championed this book early on, never forgot it, and published it the first chance she had to do so. (Has it been ten years?) Your mind and passion enriched this work.

Thank you, Andy Boyles, for asking, "What is your dream book?" and for helping strengthen the book's content at key stages. Thank you to Art Director Barbara Grzeslo, who poured skill and creativity into giving this book's design that extra zing. Thank you to my agent, Emily Mitchell of Wernick & Pratt, for keeping me percolating. Thank you to my literary lawyer, Debra Kass Orenstein. Thank you to poet/author JoAnn Early Macken, www.joannmacken.com, for help with fact-checking.

For technical assistance and review, thank you to Dr. Kim Bostwick, Senior Scientist for Public Engagement, www.birdnote.org; NASA expert/children's book author Marianne Dyson, www.Mariannedyson.com; author Karen Romano Young, www.karenromanoyoung.com; Dr. James Sweitzer, PhD, formerly of the Rose Center for Earth and Space of the American Museum of Natural History and now at Science Communications Consultants; Professor Karl Anders Ericsson of Florida State University; snail expert Marla Coppolino, www.thesnailwrangler.com; Jenny Powers and Darby Hoover of the Natural Resources Defense Council; Dr. Anette Hosoi of MIT; Professor Robert McNeill (R.M.) Alexander of the University of Leeds; Dr. Martha Weiss of Georgetown University; Sarah Freiermuth of the Coral Reef Alliance; Stephen D. Cairns, Research Scientist/Curator, Department of Zoology, Smithsonian Institution; Research Botanist Wendy C. Hodgson of the Desert Botanic Garden in Phoenix, AZ; Dr. Steven Portugal of the Structure and Motion Lab, Royal Veterinary College, University of London; Chris Sayre, and Dr. George Knowles. Every driver who has let me merge into a line of traffic, please accept a friendly wave, as well.

A slightly sleepy thank you to my husband Jeff Sayre who for years periodically dragged me out on chilly star-watching nights until I finally became interested in astronomy. I cannot imagine a finer partner for this life of delighting in nature and daily chewing over scientific mysteries.

Thank you to Lola Schaefer, Liz Cunningham, Barbara Crighton, Candace Corson, Gretchen Woelfle, Carolyn Marsden, Carmela Martino, Gretchen Will Mayo, Carolyn Crimi, Mary Ann Rodman, Jeanne Marie Grunwell, Phyllis Harris, Laura Kemp, Meribeth Shank, Jacquee Dickey, Jane Yolen, Cynthia Cotten, Jane Stemp, Virginia Koeth, the Pod, Isabel Baker, Loree Griffin Burns, the Healing Earth crew, the NatureScope crew, and all the Facebook friends who boosted my spirit through a long, slow haul. Thank you to every librarian who has ever put a quality book into the hands of someone who needed it. To all the trees that were turned into paper for this and my other books, apologies and thank you for the sacrifice.

Terry Young, thank you for supporting quality science writing and for nudging me toward doing a middle-grade science project. Thank you to Ann Rider whose comments helped this book grow during its appropriately slow journey. Thank you to Tom, Veda, Mom, Lydia, Rodney, Cathy, John, Turner, Winston, Nora, Elizabeth, Virginia, John David, Catherine, Becky, Ken, Patti, Michael, Karyn, Megan, Alexa, Kathy, Marlene and Doug Hunt, Deb the hairdresser, and Agatha the snail. Thank you, authors of the Clean Air Act and Servicemen and Servicewomen of the United States for letting me breathe in peace.

My gratitude to my grandmother and others who fought for the right for me to vote. Thank you, scientists whose hard research uncovered the information mentioned in this book. Thank you to author Jean Craighead George and her family for sharing nature and science with the world. Thank you to Tracy Burchett, one of the legion of glorious reference librarians who keep this country a democracy. To anyone who should have been listed here but wasn't, as well as anyone who actually took the time to wade through these acknowledgments, thank you for your patience and understanding.

—April Pulley Sayre, March 27, 2015

NOT-EXACTLY-THE-END-NOTES

(EXTRA NOURISHMENT FOR STICKY THINKERS AND SNAILISH SORTS)

Circling back and reexamining is natural for slow, deep thinkers. Perhaps something in this book made you wonder where in the world the information originated. Well, the ground on which this book grew was tilled, composted, and mulched by reading science news articles every morning for decades. Writing sixty books about varied topics brought the chief snail, i.e., the author, into contact with some of this material. There was also quite a bit of just staring at tree leaves and having thoughts.

That said, slow thinkers are lovers of endnotes and all kinds of itchy, complex underpinnings of bold statements. A good tangent is worth an entire day! So, in a conversational way, let's take a little journey through a bit of what I read and who I talked to as I wrote this volume. This section core samples the information-berg: it covers the more personal and substantial aspects of researching this book. (Facts that are easy to research with simple internet searches I have set aside in order to allot space to more intriguing, hard-to-find tidbits.) Enjoy the sticky journey, snail friends!

Note: Websites cited are active at time of publication. Please be aware that the particular website articles cited provide solid information but clicking on links at some websites may not be advisable.

Warning Label

Why mention giant weasels in your warning label? Well, one day when two large, black, panther-like creatures climbed down out of a tree in Panama while my husband and I were enveloped in an army-ant swarm, we thought they were about to chase us. Actually, they were more than likely just trying to get out of the way. That moment gave me a long-term fondness for giant weasels. Their common name is Tayra, scientific name *Eira barbara*, in case you want to take a look. They're actually unlikely to pursue you unless you appear to be a small rodent or piece of fruit.

CHEWY NATURE THOUGHTS

Big Tree Thoughts

My knowledge of these trees came from visiting them and the visitor center humans use to celebrate them, then rechecking official sites from the National Park Service. The blue whale metaphor was created using the weights of full-grown whales. I did not personally measure the whales because my scuba skills are not up to the task. The weights are from NOAA, the National Oceanic and Atmospheric Administration. Generally, these kinds of whale statistics are based on old whaling data. The tree age is based on studies by scientists of tree cores and tree girth. (Not all trees were cored. A few core samples were taken for comparison.) A few of the 14 sources used are listed below.

"*Sequoiadendron giganteum.*"
US Forestry Service. Web. 20 Mar. 2015. www.fs.fed.us/database/feis/plants/tree/seqgig/all.html.
"The Giant Sequoia (*Sequoiadendron giganteum*), the Biggest Tree in the World." *Monumental Trees, an Inventory of Big and Old Trees Worldwide.* Web. 20 Mar. 2015. www.monumentaltrees.com/en/trees/giantsequoia/giantsequoia/.

Stephenson, Nathan L. "Estimated Ages of Some Large Giant Sequoias: General Sherman Keeps Getting Younger" *U.S. Geological Survey. Madroño,* Vol 47, No.1, Pp. 61-67, 1 Jan. 2000. Web. 20 Mar. 2015. www.nps.gov/yose/learn/nature/upload/Sequoia-aging-2000.pdf.
"NEFSC Fish FAQ." *NEFSC Fish FAQ.* Web. 20 Mar. 2015. www.nefsc.noaa.gov/faq/fishfaq9.html.

Coral Brains and Coral Ages

Various articles quote the work of paleoceanographer E. Brendan Roark, then at Stanford University, who was working with a team using radiocarbon dating to find the age of corals that grow off the coast of Oahu, Hawaii. Coral is not a single species but many species, so statistics about coral growth per year varied widely in the scientific articles I read. After tracking down dozens of figures, I settled on a broader statement to show their slow growth—the fraction of an inch/few millimeters per year statement. Figures about the specific brain coral size came from general websites about the island of Tobago. Two coral scientists reviewed the text I wrote.

If you want to ponder deeply, research the age of not just corals, but coral reefs. I had to delete an entire section from the book because the research on that issue was so confusing, as answers ranged from 5 thousand to 30 thousand to 120 million years or more.

Etnoyer, Peter. "World's Oldest Animal Aged to 4000 Years." *Deep Sea News*. Web. 02 Feb 2008. www.deepseanews.com/2008/02/worlds-oldest-animal-aged-to-4000-years/

Roark, E. Brendan. "Extreme Longevity in Proteinaceous Deep-sea Corals." PNAS, 10 Oct. 2008. Web. 06 Aug. 2015. www.pnas.org/content/early/2009/03/20/0810875106.abstract

SeaWeb. "Living Corals Thousands Of Years Old Hold Clues To Past Climate Changes." ScienceDaily. ScienceDaily, 19 February 2008. www.sciencedaily.com/releases/2008/02/080214130404.htm.

Moth Memories

Multiple articles, including the one below, describe the moth memory work of Martha Weiss. After writing an initial draft for that section, in March of 2014, I communicated with her by e-mail in order to make sure I had properly represented her work.

Jabr, Ferris. "How Does a Caterpillar Turn into a Butterfly?" *Scientific American Global RSS*. Scientific American, Inc., 10 Aug. 2012. Web. 21 Mar. 2015. www.scientificamerican.com/article/caterpillar-butterfly-metamorphosis-explainer/.

It's About Time

This section grew from a conversation my husband and I had in 2002 with a time-perception scientist who was dining at the same table with us at a Peruvian rainforest ecolodge. We were all so exhausted from hiking around and looking at giant Amazon River otters that I took notes from our talk but never asked his name.

Here is my advice to you: write fascinating people's names and contact information in your little notebooks as soon as you can politely do so. You never know when you may want to track down that person because you might put something related in a manuscript and that manuscript might be published—oh, say, fourteen years later.

Now, let's move onward to discuss how time passes for flies and nonfiction authors. First, let me tell you from experience that if you're researching a hot topic in science, you may read a dozen web articles about a subject. Yet when you dig more deeply, you'll often find that they're all just interpreting and rewording a single, recent scientific article. That was the case with body size and time perception in 2013. Most were just drilling down into the Kevin Healy research listed below. (I'm not saying re-interpretation is unimportant. The Alger article, for instance, does a great job of illuminating the research in relation to other science.)

Of the general articles I read about studies of time passing, the one that grabbed me was the Halberg one about timing how long it took a single minute to pass.

Alger, Sarah Jane. "Metabolism and Body Size Influence the Perception of Movement and Time." Nature. com. Nature Publishing Group, 30 Dec. 2013. Web. www.nature.com/ scitable/blog/accumulating-glitches/metabolism_and_body_ size_influence.

Healy, Kevin. "Metabolic Rate and Body Size Are Linked with Perception of Temporal Information." Science Direct. Animal Behavior, Volume 86, Issue 4, Pages 685-696, 1 Oct. 2013. Web. www.sciencedirect.com/science/ article/pii/S0003347213003060.

Halberg, Franz, Robert Sothern, Germaine Cornélissen, and Jerzy Czaplicki. "Chronomics, Human Time Estimation, and Aging." *Clinical Interventions in Aging.* *2008 Dec; 3(4):* 749-760. Dove Medical Press, 3 Dec. 2008. Web. www.ncbi.nlm.nih.gov/pmc/articles/ PMC2662403/.

Most of the dozen other scientific articles I read (not listed here) were to help me understand Critical Flicker Fusion (CFF). Critical Flicker Fusion is the kind of catchy phrase a person wants to digest before tossing it around while having sandwiches with scientists. (Advice: make the sandwiches yourself. Scientists are sometimes too busy with big thoughts to notice what they put between pieces of bread.)

Here's why CFF is important: It's not easy to ask a squirrel or a fruit fly deep questions about how they experience time. So, instead, scientists measure an animal's critical flicker fusion. That's the rate at which a flickering light starts to look like a steady beam, at least to the test subject's eyes.

First, the scientists reward an animal, such as a chicken or honeybee, for choosing either a flickering image or a still one until they've trained the animal to always choose the correct image. Then, the scientists vary the frequency of the flickering image until they find a point where the animal cannot tell which image is flickering and which is not.

That point, the speed at which images flick from dark to light to dark, indicates how fast a motion the animal can see. This gives scientists some idea whether the animal perceives actions in slow motion, which may indicate how they experience the world around them.

Did you have to read this CFF passage several times to understand it? I had to do the same thing with the CFF articles I read, too.

Another Slow Thing to Think About

What about decay? Well, decay is a messy field of study, indeed. I wasted (pun intended) many hours trying to track down the sources for internet lists of how long it takes various kinds of garbage to decay, since the lists often disagreed with one another. I called several website sources and no one seemed to know where they found a lot of this information. (Much of a nonfiction author's time is spent rooting around in endnotes and footnotes and tracking sources. Footnotes help me recheck facts and wander down trails to additional information. I often find experts in a field by reading the lists of papers that scientists quote.) There is some reason for the decay figures to disagree, of course. As I learned from Darby Hoover, decay varies a lot according to conditions. Plus, we just don't know yet how long it takes for some newer materials to decay. That makes me wonder if some of these "estimates" are more like wild guesses. Oh, well. I wanted to finish this book, and present its other subjects before I myself

decayed, so I cut the unsupported decay times from my list.

SLOW ANIMALS
Snail Stuff

For the garden snail speed, I went out in the garden, put a piece of paper in front of a snail and timed how long it took it to travel. No, when I was an eight-year-old girl, I did not know I would grow up to have a job that included timing snail locomotion. Sometimes life is just awesome like that. While at Duke University, I did study leech locomotion but unfortunately the leech escaped in my dorm room and was never found. My human roommate was not amused by that research misadventure.

I learned about Robosnails from a variety of popular science articles. Direct correspondence with the scientist, Dr. Anette Hosoi of Massachusetts Institute of Technology, during March of 2008 enhanced that initial research.

The discovery that the sea snail's radula is strong comes from recent articles, including the one listed below this section. (Note that it's not just any sea snail, it's a limpet! Anyone else besides me think limpets are totally cool? I spent many childhood hours with my friend Miranda studying seashells of all sorts.)

The information about snail wrangler Marla Coppolino came from direct correspondence with her in May of 2014. You can find out more about her, her work, and her presentations at www.thesnailwrangler.com.

Agatha the snail and the snail mail e-mail had nothing to do with this book. It's just that my husband and I have a fondness for snails, and keep our eyes out for news on them, perhaps because we coauthored a book called *One Is a Snail, Ten Is a Crab*. The snail mail was an intriguing use of science so my husband sent me an e-mail in this way. Yes, we find that kind of thing entertaining.

You, too, will doubtless find snails entertaining if you read the work of Dr. Tim Pierce, Assistant Curator of Mollusks at the Carnegie Museum of Natural History. He's making me want to write a book entirely about snails—watch out! If you want to disappear into land snail study, check out www.carnegiemnh.org/science/mollusks/.

Oskin, Becky. "Sorry, Spiders: Sea Snails Make Strongest Material on Earth." LiveScience. TechMedia Network, 17 Feb. 2015. Web. www.livescience.com/49844-limpet-teeth-strongest-natural-material.html.
Sayre, April Pulley, and Jeff Sayre. *One Is a Snail, Ten Is a Crab: A Counting by Feet Book*. Cambridge, Mass.: Candlewick, 2003. Print.

Slowworms

Slowworms are covered quite well in typical internet articles on science sites. The BBC site below has some rather gooey video of slowworms being born. JPR, an environmental consulting company, mentions creating "hibernacula" for slowworms. Just say the word and wonder over it or read the article listed below:

"Nature Wildlife: Slow Worms." *BBC News*. BBC, 1 Oct. 2014. Web. 21 Mar. 2015. www.bbc.co.uk/nature/life/Anguis_fragilis#p003k8hc.
"Slow-worm Habitat, Ecology, Mitigation and Fencing." JPR Environmental. Web. 21 Mar. 2015. www.jprenvironmental.co.uk/protected_species_profile_slow_worm.htm.

Flapping and Flying

One Ohio evening my husband and I squatted in the wet grass with esteemed bird guides from around the world as we listened to a single male woodcock's wings whistle as it circled above our heads. It then landed right in front of us and walked around with its seemingly impossibly big bill. Witnessing this bird's display was simultaneously sacred and comical. As lifelong birders, we've traveled to see many of the flappers mentioned in this book, including albatrosses taking off from cliffs in the Galapagos Islands.

But just because you have seen something does not mean you truly know it. The information about flight speeds and flapping came from a large number of papers; the one below was the most substantial. I reconfirmed this information through correspondence with Dr. Steven Portugal, who studies how much energy birds use as they flap. Although it was not a source for this book, a fun follow up site for students and teachers intrigued by flapping and other kinds of flight can be found at www.ornithopter.org/birdflight/index.shtml

Pennycuick, C.J. "Wingbeat Frequency of Birds in Steady Cruising Flight: New Data and Improved Predictions." *Journal of Experimental Biology*, 21 Mar. 1996. Web. 21 Mar. 2015. jeb.biologists.org/content/199/7/1613.full.pdf.

Slow Animals

The slow statistics were obtained in an exchange of e-mails I had with Professor Robert McNeill Alexander, a renowned British Zoologist from the University of Leeds on March 21, 2008. He has done decades of research in the field of biomechanics, which is the study of how animals move. An authority not just in tiny creature locomotion, but also dinosaur locomotion, Alexander worked on a formula to figure out, based on the length of leg bones and the size of tracks, how quickly dinosaurs likely moved.

The octopus mother was featured in the article listed below. Alas, mother octopuses don't live to raise their young.

Schrope, Mark. "'Octomom' Sets Gestation Record: Deep-sea Octopus Broods Eggs for More than Four Years." Nature.com. Nature Publishing Group, 30 July 2014. Web. www.nature.com/news/octomom-sets-gestation-record-1.15646.

Cow Magnets

General information about cow magnets is fairly widespread but if you want to read more gruesome details, you can chew over the following article, which was written by a veterinarian. He's written several articles about cow stomachs on the same site, with titles that include "Why pop cans and cattle don't mix," and "A cow's stomach is one of the wonders of nature." Now there is a fellow who ruminates on ruminants.

Croushore, Bill. "'Hardware Disease' Isn't Fun for the Cow or Veterinarian." *DailyAmerican.com*. 18 Apr. 2011. Web. 22 Mar. 2015. articles.dailyamerican.com/2011-04-18/opinion/29445865_1_hardware-disease-cow-magnet.

Sea Slugs

Obsessed with sea slugs? You're in luck. Articles about research on sea slugs called *Aplysia* are coming out thick and fast, even as this book is going to press. The 2000 Nobel Prize in Physiology or Medicine went to neuroscientist Dr. Eric Kandel, a professor from Columbia University who studies memory formation in sea slugs and humans. These articles, alas, are on popular sites whose web links seem to break almost as soon as I list them. So, instead I recommend that sea slug science fans whet their appetites by looking at the Whitney laboratory website listed below.

In addition, whether you're interested in sea slugs or sassafras trees, a good way to search for meaty scientific articles, not just popular articles, is to use Google Scholar instead of Google Search. It helps if you search by a species's scientific name, not just its common name. Don't worry if you do not understand every word of each article. Dictionaries help. You'll get used to reading scientific papers and feel brainy and fabulous after doing so.

"Current Projects." The Whitney Laboratory for Marine Bioscience. Web. 23 Mar. 2015. www.whitney. ufl.edu/research/faculty/leonid-l-moroz.

SLOW PLANTS

I researched slow growing plants such as the century plant, saguaro, and bristlecone pine on standard science and National Park Service websites. (Wendy Hodgsen of the Desert Botanic Garden in Phoenix helped confirm facts.) Old tree fans might want to check out the more unusual sources below. Apparently, scientists keep databases of information about ancient trees. Perhaps some grow near you.

"OldList: A Database of Ancient Trees." *Rocky Mountain Tree-Ring Research, OLDLIST.* Web. 22 Mar. 2015. www.rmtrr.org/oldlist.htm.

"Eastern OLDLIST: A Database of Maximum Tree Ages for Eastern North America." *Eastern OLDLIST: A Database of Maximum Tree Ages for Eastern North America.* Tree Ring Laboratory of Lamont-Doherty Earth Observatory and Columbia University. Web. 1 Jan. 2015. www.ldeo.columbia.edu/~adk/oldlisteast/.

Sussman, Rachel, and Hans Ulrich Obrist. *The Oldest Living Things in the World.* Chicago: Chicago University Press, 2014. Print.

SLOW BODY THOUGHTS

Water and Breathing

Information about human biology, such as how many breaths humans take and how much water is inside a human, is strangely easier to find than information on snails. (Why?) Here are just a fraction of the human body sources:

"The Water in You." *Water Properties: (Water Science for Schools)*. United States Geological Survey, 17 Mar. 2014. Web. www.water.usgs.gov/edu/propertyyou.html.

Lewis, III, MD, James L. "About Body Water." *Water Balance: Merck Manual Home Edition*. Merck. Web. 22 Jan. 2015. www.merckmanuals.com/home/hormonal_and_metabolic_disorders/water_balance/about_body_water.html.

Richter, Brian. "Walking Water: H2O and the Human Body." *National Geographic Blog*. 6 Mar. 2012. Web. www.newswatch.nationalgeographic.com/2012/03/06/human-body-water/.

Sleep Information

Information about sleepers remembering words was from research described in the BBC article below. The 90-minute cycle in daytime and nighttime activities is based on the work of Nathaniel Kleitman, a sleep research pioneer who created the idea of BRAC, the Basic Rest–Activity Cycle. Many researchers found cycles roughly 90 minutes long but there are overlapping cycles. This field of inquiry sounds simple in popularized science articles but the underlying studies are vastly complex.

One of the more useful and in-depth sleep articles, among the dozens I read, is the National Institutes of Health's Teacher's Guide to Sleep. (Note that it's not instructions for how teachers should sleep, but how teachers should teach about sleep.) It explains relevant processes and even has a nifty table of animal sleep requirements so you can look up how long a goat or a hamster or your local teenager should sleep, on average.

"Brain Can Classify Words During Sleep." BBC News. 11 Sept. 2014. Web. /www.bbc.com/news/health-29166466.

"Brain Basics: Understanding Sleep." National Institute of Neurological Disorders and Stroke (NINDS). National Institutes of Health, 25 July 2014. Web. www.ninds.nih.gov/disorders/brain_basics/understanding_sleep.htm.

Kleitman, Nathaniel. "Basic Rest-Activity Cycle—22 Years Later." Sleep, 5(4) 311-317, 1 Jan. 1982. Web. www.journalsleep.org/ViewAbstract.aspx?pid=25389.

Peretsman, Natalie. "What Happens to Your Body When You Fall Asleep?" Scienceline. 6 Feb. 2008. Web. scienceline.org/2008/02/ask-peretsman-sleep/.

"Sleep, Sleep Disorders, and

Biological Rhythms." Teacher's Guide: Information about Sleep. National Institutes of Health. Web. 1 Jan. 2015. www.science. education.nih.gov/supplements/ nih3/sleep/guide/info-sleep.html.

ROCK ON!
Geological Thoughts Worth Savoring

Below are a few of the slow geology articles I read. So many rocks, so little time. Actually, so much time . . . the age of the Grand Canyon has been a matter of debate. The idea that it was several canyons that merged to form one canyon 6 million years ago, was published in recent research. Parts of the canyon are much older, 50–70 million years old. That's even more box turtle lifetimes! (By the way, fossil remains indicate turtles were here with the dinosaurs and even before the oldest parts of the Grand Canyon formed.)

Granite erosion, too, has its backstory. How quickly it erodes depends on conditions. In dry, cold conditions it can erode less than a yard (one meter) per million years. But in very humid, warm conditions, it can erode as quickly as 2–22 yards (2–20 meters) in a million years.

Figures for the widening of the Mid-Atlantic Ridge vary in popular science articles. That is because the plates pull apart at different rates at different locations along the seam between the plates. The United States Geological Service indicates that each year the Mid-Atlantic Ridge separates at about an inch (2.5 centimeters), on average.

Bierman, Paul. "How Quickly Does Granite Erode? Evidence From Analyses of In Situ Produced 10-Be, 26-A1, And 36-C1." *Department of Geology, University of Vermont.* University of Vermont, 1 Jan. 1995. Web.

Kerr, Richard A. "The Grand Canyon as Frankenstein." *The Grand Canyon as Frankenstein.* Science, 26 Jan. 2014. Web. www.news.sciencemag. org/earth/2014/01/grand-canyon-frankenstein.

Meierding, Thomas C. "Marble Tombstone Weathering and Air Pollution in North America." *Annals of the Association of American Geographers* (1993): 568–88. Print.

"Understanding Plate Motions [This Dynamic Earth, USGS]." 15 Sep. 2014. www.pubs.usgs.gov/publications/test/understanding.html

Yeager, Ashley. "Grand Canyon's Origin Dated to 6 Million Years Ago." *Science News.* 26 Jan. 2014. Web. www.sciencenews.org/blog/science-ticker/grand-canyons-origin-dated-6-million-years-ago.

"When Did the Statue of Liberty Turn Green?" NYC Media, *New-York Historical Society*. Web. 12 January 2012. www.nyhistory.org/community/when-did-the-statue-of-liberty-turn-green.

SLOW STUFF

Eighteen years ago my husband and I were learning to record sounds in a rain forest in Ecuador. As it rained and my glasses fogged up, I kept looking back down the forest road. I thought a truck must be nearby because I could hear its *beep, beep, beep,* as it was backing up. Moments later we learned the sound source was much smaller: it was the club-winged manakin, doing its courtship display. Fast forward almost two decades, and I read about scientist Kim Bostwick, who, with the help of high speed video cameras, has found out how the birds make this goofy sound. Her website, singingwings.org has videos and other information beyond what you can find in popular science magazine articles. Her research on manakins has been featured widely on videos and television shows. (One species of manakin became a Youtube sensation because of the slow-motion "moonwalk" in its courtship display.)

As for the other slow stuff, yes, I really did call McDonalds to find out how quickly they cook their food, and really did read scientific articles on raisin drying. (Hands-on research is good, and I would've tried putting out grapes to dry, but realistically, the neighborhood squirrels would have eaten them.) In case you just need a "raisin" to read, try *The Raisin Production Manual.*

Christensen, L. Peter, and William L. Peacock. "The Raisin Drying Process." *Raisin Production Manual* (2000): 207–216. Print.

SLOW ART

For the project to make John Cage's music last 639 years, there are articles in the *Washington Post* and *Huffington Post*, and a radio story on National Public Radio. The official website of the project is www.aslsp.org but heads up: it's in German.

Another heap of research went into finding out about Lorenzo Ghiberti, who spent decades creating doors for the Battistero di San Giovanni in Florence, Italy. Poor fellow—his section, like so many others, was cut from this book. Thankfully, his gorgeous doors remain to tell about his work even if I cannot.

Paint drying research came from artist friends and even the websites of paint companies. I was a bit worried about the articles on Keith Jackson's job watching paint dry because the sources were British publications, and I do not know which are tabloids with questionable standards for news, and which are reliable in their reporting. So, I tracked down the technical sales director at AquaTec Coatings, the company that employed Keith Jackson, and asked him by e-mail. He confirmed that Jackson had been employed there and that, yes, his job really had been to watch paint dry.

Mount Rushmore is a national park and is covered well in government websites, PBS stories, and NPR stories. The Crazy Horse Memorial has a website, www.crazyhorsememorial. org.

You'd think something like the Great Wall of China, which has been around for thousands of years, would not change much in a decade or so. But between the time I started writing this book and the time that it was published, it did! Fortunately, my daily reading of science headlines caught the recent study of the Great Wall and its newly surveyed length.

By the way, many articles incorrectly state that astronauts can easily see the Great Wall from space. Wrong! (And I should know. I almost put that error in this book.) Apparently, you need a pretty good camera to zoom in, plus a lot of time on your hands to peer at photos to look for the Great Wall and even then, you might not see it. The NASA article below discusses this and some human-built structures that you can see from space with just your eyes and no special equipment such as a camera or binoculars. Of course, I do recommend you use special equipment such as a space capsule to get to space and stay alive out there, even if you do not bring binoculars.

As for Slow Television, it has been covered in the United States press but the most fun is the actual Norwegian site run by the television station that produces the programming: www.nrk. no/presse/slow-tv-1.12057032 I'm a tad disappointed that the National Knitting Night received a higher rating than 24 hours of scientists lecturing. But the train journey and salmon stream sound interesting. At the bottom of that page are links to articles about Slow TV. By the way, Slow TV programming is apparently coming to some United States cable channels, as well.

"China's Wall Less Great in View From Space." *NASA*. Ed. John Ira Petty. 9 May 2005. Web. www.nasa.gov/vision/space/workinginspace/great_wall.html.

Judkis, Maura. "World's Longest Concert Will Last 639 Years." *Washington Post*. 28 Nov. 2011.

MORE SLOW THOUGHTS: OUTER SPACE

I mention that we are seeing the past when we see the light of stars. Well, strictly speaking, even when you look at a lamp, you're seeing the past, too. That's because light from everything takes a while to travel to your eyes. But it only takes a tiny fraction of time to travel from a lamp to you. The dark matter quotes from Dr. James S. Sweitzer, PhD, then at the Rose Center for Earth and Space at the American Museum of Natural History, were from e-mails we exchanged in January of 2002; I reconfirmed this information with him earlier this year.

Marianne Dyson, a former NASA flight controller who is herself an acclaimed children's book author, helped me weed out some misconceptions from the space text. All the other materials came from standard sources such as NASA websites. The Voyager site below has a counter that updates Voyager 1 and Voyager 2's distance from Earth. Feel free to have some fun with math and calculations using the various numbers on that site.

If you're getting starry-eyed, check out the Star Walk app and dig in deeper with the yearly *Astronomical Calendar* created by Guy Ottewell. It is science and art.

Ottewell, Guy. *Astronomical Calendar*. Greenville: Astronomical Workshop, 2015. Print.

"Voyager—The Interstellar Mission." Voyager—The Interstellar Mission. Web. 27 Mar. 2015. www.voyager.jpl. nasa.gov.

I hope these resources have satisfied at least a little bit of your hunger, oh sloth-arm-reachers who tend to pull down books from upper shelves. My advice is to go out and spend your money on some field guides. Try field guides to fungi, caterpillars, seashells, stars—whatever catches your heart and mind. Slow-moving observers often need to pause in paths and browse such books. Carry a field guide in your backpack or build a pile next to a comfy seat where you can rediscover the books and browse them, again and again.

So, how does one trail off and end an endnote? Of course!

THE OTHER END

INDEX

A

acid rain, 150
acrylic paint, 111
Aesop's fables, 37
agave plant. *See* century plant
aging, time and, 19
Alzheimer's disease, 59, 150
animals, slow, 24–59, 162
    colonial, 12, 150
    how scientists test slow motion in, 159–160
    marine, 48–49
    slow creature statistics, 51
AquaTec Coatings, 112, 167
architects, 150
art, 106–109
    paintings, 111
"As Slow as Possible" (Cage), 108–109
astrobiologists, 143, 150
astrophysicists, 138, 144, 150

B

balloons, hot air, 10
Barber, Asa, 30–31
BBC, 161
biodegradability, 23, 50

biodiversity, 98, 150
birds
    Bostwick study of, 102–103
    manakins, 102–103, 166
    moonwalking, 102–103, 166
    slowest-flying, 40–45
    slow motion video of, 102–103
    web site on flapping and flight of, 162
    wing beats of, 44–45
    with largest wingspan, 46–47
    woodcocks, 40–41, 161
black corals, 12
bodies, human, 72–95
    breathing and, 76–77, 163–164
    rhythms in, 80–81
    sleep and, 78–83, 164
    water in, 74–75
Bonaparte, Napoleon, 119
Bonsai trees, 114–115
books, oldest surviving, 10
Bostwick, Kim, 102–103, 166
bottles, glass, 20–21
brain corals, 12, 157–158
brain, during sleep, 78
breathing, 76–77, 163–164
bristlecone pines, 68–69, 163
buildings, 118–119

C

cacti, saguaro, 66–67, 163
Cage, John, 108–109, 167
caterpillars, 14–15
cathedral, Duomo of Milan, 119
cells, 10, 150
century plants, 64–65, 163
CFF. See Critical Flicker Fusion
ciliate, 150
cocoon, 14, 151
colonial animals, 12, 150
Colorado River, 86
comets, 74, 150
composers, 150
continental plates, 94
Copernicus, Nicholaus, 10
Coppolino, Marla, 35, 160
corals
　　black, 12
　　brain, 12, 157–158
　　polyps, 13
　　reef-building, 49
cows
　　hardware disease in, 56–57, 162
　　magnets in, 56–57, 162
cranes, 44
Crazy Horse Memorial, 116–117, 167
Critical Flicker Fusion (CFF), 159–160
crust, Earth's, 94, 150
cud, 56

D

dark matter, 144, 168
da Saluzzo, Antonio (archbishop), 119
decay, 20–22, 160

decomposition, 21–22, 151
dinosaurs, 10
Duomo of Milan (cathedral), 119

E

Earth
　　continental plates of, 94
　　crust of, 94, 150
　　sun and, 140
　　water on, 74–75, 163–164
e-mail, snail mail experiment with, 36, 161
engineers, 26, 30, 151
Eta Carinae, 133
exercise, 83

F

falcons, peregrine, 41
fast food, 98–99
fermentation, 151
films, slow motion, 100–101
　　imaginary, 125
fingernails, 94–95
flagellates, 151
flies, 16
flight, websites on wing flapping and, 162
food, 98–99

G

galaxy
　　defined, 140
　　spiral shape of, 140
garbologists, 22, 151
garden snails, 24–25, 160

gastropods, 30, 151
genes, 13, 59, 151
geology, 84–95, 165–166
    geological defined, 151
ginkgo trees, 128, 151
glands, 151
glass bottles, 20–21
Google Scholar, 163
Grand Canyon, 86–87
granite
    erosion, 165
    mountains, 90–91
grapes, 99
graveyards, 92–93
The Great Wall of China, 120–121, 167

H

Halberg, Franz, 159
hardware disease, in cows, 56–57, 162
hares, 37
Healy, Kevin, 158
Hooke, Robert, 10
Hoover, Darby, 21, 160
Hosoi, Anette, 26, 160
hot air balloons, 10
Hubble Space Telescope, 136–137
humans. See also bodies, human
    gene similarity between sea slugs
    and, 59
    skulls of, 72
    twin, 13
hummingbirds, 42–43

I

innards, 56, 151
interstellar space, 138, 151

J

jack-in-the-pulpit plant, 64
Jackson, Keith, 112
Jackson, Michael, 103
Jefferson, Thomas, 116–117

K

Kandel, Eric, 163
kilometer, 151

L

landfills, 22–23
landmarks, 88–89
librarian, 152
    reference, 153
life, conditions for existence of, 140–141
life-forms, on other planets, 142–143
light-years, 132–136
limpets, 160
Lincoln, Abraham, 116–117
locomotion, 152

M

magnets, cow, 56–57, 162
manakins, 102–103, 166
mangroves, 63, 152
marine animals, slowest, 48–49
Matthaei Botanical Gardens, 64
maturity, 152

mayflies, 16
McDonald's, 99
Meierding, Tom, 92–93
memories, moth, 14–15, 158
Mendeleev, Dimitri, 10
Methuselah tree, 68–69
microscopes, 52–53
Mid-Atlantic Ridge, 94–95, 165
migration, snail, 32–35
Milky Way Galaxy, 140
modern life, 96–97
moisture, 152
mollusks, 152, 161
molten rock, 152
moths, memories of, 14–15, 158
mountains, 11, 90–91
Mount Rushmore, 116–117, 167
movies, slow motion, 100–101
    imaginary, 125
mucus, 26, 153
mull, 152
music, 108–109
    rest in, 108, 153

N
"National Firewood Night," 122
National Oceanic and Atmospheric
    Administration (NOAA), 157
nematodes, 50–51
NOAA. See National Oceanic and
    Atmospheric Administration
North Star, 133

O
ocean, basin of, 94, 152
octopuses, 54–55
oil paint, 111
The Oldest Living Things in the World
    (Sussman), 69
organism, 152
ornithologists, 102, 152
outer space, 131–147, 167
    interstellar space, 138, 151
ovoviviparous, 38–39
oxygen, 77

P
paint drying, 111–113, 166–167
paintings, 111
Parkinson's disease, 59, 153
patina, 88–89
pennies, gathering, 128
peregrine falcon, 41
periwinkles, 148, 153
Pierse, Tim, 161
pine trees, bristlecone, 68–69, 163
planets, life-forms on other, 142–143
plants, slow, 61–68, 163
    ancient, 69
    century, 64–65, 163
    movement in, 62–63
plastic trash, 23
polyps
    coral, 13
    defined, 153
ponderings, 153
Portugal, Steven, 162
protozoans, 51, 153
Proxima Centauri, 133

R

radish, 64
radula, snail, 30, 161
rain, acid, 150
raisins, 99, 166
reference librarian, 153
resources, 156–168
rest
    in music, 108, 153
    pages for, 148–149
Robosnails, 26–27, 160
rocks, 165–166
    molten, 152
    weathering process of, 92–93
Roosevelt, Theodore, 116–117
roundworms (nematodes), 50–51

S

saguaro cacti, 66–67, 163
salmon, 122–123
sculpture, Crazy Horse, 116–117, 167
sea horses, 49
sea slugs, 59, 163
sea snails, 30, 153, 160, 161
sea sponges, 128
sequoia trees, 11
sheep, counting, 125
Sierra Nevada mountains, 11
skull, human, 72
sleep, 78–83, 164
    brain during, 78
    cycles, 80–81
sloths, 56
slow days, 104–105
Slow Food Foundation for Biodiversity, 98

slow motion, 100–103, 125, 159–160
slow things to try, 128–129
slow worms, 38–39, 161
slugs, sea, 59, 163
snail mail, 36, 161
snails
    classification of, 30
    definition of, 153
    migration, 32–35
    radula of, 30, 161
    Robosnails, 26–27, 160
    sea, 30, 59, 153, 160, 161, 163
    speed of garden, 24–25, 160
    teeth of, 30–31
snail wrangler, 35, 160
solar system, 153
space. See outer space
spaghetti sauce, 99
species, 153
    coral and, 157
    researching on, 163
stars, 132–133, 140, 168
statistics, slow creature, 51
Statue of Liberty, 88–89, 166
stories, telling slow, 124
studying, 129
sun, 133, 140
Sussman, Rachel, 69
Sweitzer, James S., 144, 168

T

t'ai chi, 83, 153
tectonic plates, 94
telescopes, Hubble Space, 136–137
television, slow, 122–123, 167
tendril, 153

time, 16–19, 159–160
tinkerer, 153
tombstones, 92–93
tortoises, 37, 51
trash, 23
trees
    ancient, 68
    Bonsai, 114–115
    bristlecone pines, 68–69, 163
    core samples, 157
    ginkgo, 128, 151
    Methuselah, 68–69
    sequoia, 11
turkey vultures, 44–45
twins, human, 13

U

universe
    dark matter in, 144, 168
    expansion of, 146–147
universities, first, 10

V

videos, slow motion, 102–103
Voyager 1, 10, 138–139, 168–169
Voyager 2, 10, 138–139, 168–169
vultures, turkey, 44–45

W

walking, 83
    moon-, 102–103, 166
Washington, George, 116–117
water, 74–75, 163–164

weasels, 156
Weiss, Martha, 14–15, 158
whales, 11, 50, 157
Whitney Laboratory, 163
woodcocks, 40–41, 161
worms
    nematode, 50–51
    slow, 38–39, 161

Z

Ziolkowski, Korczak, 116

APRIL PULLEY SAYRE is an award-winning author of more than 60 science books, including the popular *Rah, Rah, Radishes!*; *Stars Beneath Your Bed: The Surprising Story of Dust* (an ALA Notable Book); and *Vulture View*, which received a Theodor Seuss Geisel Honor Award. She reads science articles and stares at stars and snails in Indiana. aprilsayre.com

KELLY MURPHY has illustrated numerous picture books and chapter books, including *Face Bug*, the *New York Times* Best Seller *Masterpiece*, and the Nathaniel Fludd, Beastologist book series. She teaches at the Rhode Island School of Design and lives in Providence, Rhode Island. kelmurphy.com

31901060376300